THRILLING TALES OF THE MONTROSE SEARCH AND RESCUE

THRILLING TALES OF
THE MONTROSE SEARCH AND RESCUE

MIKE LAWLER

All photos provided by the
Montrose Search and Rescue Team

Dedicated to the husbands, wives, partners, and children (and even grandchildren!) of the Montrose Search and Rescue Team members, who have to wait behind and worry as the team members risk their lives to save others. The royalties from this book are being donated to the Montrose Search and Rescue Team.

America Through Time is an imprint of Fonthill Media LLC
www.through-time.com
office@through-time.com

Published by Arcadia Publishing by arrangement with Fonthill Media LLC
For all general information, please contact Arcadia Publishing:
Telephone: 843-853-2070
Fax: 843-853-0044
E-mail: sales@arcadiapublishing.com
For customer service and orders:
Toll-Free 1-888-313-2665

www.arcadiapublishing.com

First published 2018

Copyright © Mike Lawler 2018

ISBN 978-1-63499-077-6

All rights reserved. No part of this publication may be reproduced, stored in a retrieval system or transmitted in any form or by any means, electronic, mechanical, photocopying, recording or otherwise, without prior permission in writing from Fonthill Media LLC

Typeset in Mrs Eaves XL Serif Narrow
Printed and bound in England

Contents

Foreword	7
The History of the Montrose Search and Rescue Team—Our Local Heroes	9
Mountain Rescues	17
Ice and Snow Rescues	44
Car Crash Rescues	57
Dog Rescues	69
Plane Crash Rescues	76
Underground Rescues	84
The Lighter Side of Rescues	95
Bibliography	112

Steve Goldsworthy on patrol in the Angeles National Forest.

Foreword

Why do we do volunteer our time on the rescue team? Why get woken up by a pager, maybe miss a day of work, just to help someone you have never met?

Flash back to Christmas day, six p.m., and we are sitting down to Christmas dinner. Yes, off goes the pager and several members of the Montrose Search and Rescue Team head up the hill to save two young women stuck on a cliff face 500 feet above the canyon bottom. I think I got home and into bed about 3 a.m. the next morning.

But again, why do we this? About a month after the Christmas dinner call, we were helping with an animal rescue when I came across a hiker who had taken a shortcut. That hiker found the ID of a young woman who had disappeared three years before. She was well known and had many friends in our community and we had searched for her many times. That hiker also found what was later identified as her car, about 600 feet over the side of Angeles Crest Highway. That call would turn into three days of searching and recovering her remains.

At our next meeting her family came to give us their thanks. Her son, who was three when she disappeared, and now six, gave us a card he had written. On the outside is a picture of him with his mom. On the inside he wrote "Thank you for finding my mommy. Now I know where she is, she is in heaven watching over me."

And that is really why we do what we do.

Steve Goldsworthy, Montrose Search and Rescue Team

The History of the Montrose Search and Rescue Team—Our Local Heroes

We live on the doorstep of a massive wilderness, the Angeles National Forest. This vast mountainous area is crisscrossed with miles of twisting, narrow mountain roads, and a confusing maze of hiking trails. The hundreds of square miles of nearly vertical mountainsides and deep ravines are made up of fractured and decomposing granite rock, which slides and falls regularly, making for some of the most treacherous hiking in the world. To add to that, this wilderness is immediately adjacent to a huge city, with millions of people seeking recreation. This combination ensures that nearly every weekend, nearly every day in fact, some fragile human is going to get lost, drive off a mountainside, get trapped in snow, or all three. In addition, the mountains are riddled with abandoned mines that call out to ill-advised thrill-seekers and are crisscrossed by thousands of airplanes that occasionally fall prey to gravity and make unscheduled landings. Our giving and generous community has responded to this by volunteering to rescue these people. In fact, we have a group dedicated to just that task: the Montrose Search and Rescue Team.

The Montrose Search and Rescue Team is one of the premier search and rescue teams in Southern California. They are one of the best, and one of the first, if not the first such organized units in California. They trace their beginnings back to the dark days of WWII, when the Pacific Coast expected to be attacked by the Japanese at any moment. In early 1942, just after Pearl Harbor, the Montrose Sheriff Station was designated as the headquarters for the Air Raid Wardens program. Volunteers from the community flocked to the program to provide rescue services and fire suppression for the expected bombings. But as the war progressed and attacks became less likely, the air wardens busied themselves with mountain rescues. When the war ended, these local volunteers found that they had enjoyed the training and comradery, enjoyed the rescues they had performed, and they didn't want to disband. Nor did the county want to lose these dedicated volunteers. So, the county reformed them into Auxiliary Deputy Sheriffs, with an official mission as a disaster law enforcement organization.

Interestingly enough, the team's development was inextricably tied to the completion of the Angeles Crest Highway. In 1946 construction began anew on Angeles Crest Highway. As this major highway pushed further into the wilderness, the team got busier and busier with mountain rescues. In 1947 the Lion's Club bought the team a jeep, along with a trailer full of rescue supplies. By 1950, it was decided to fully deputize the volunteers, and the newly named Sheriff Emergency Reserve team was issued badges.

The Angeles Crest Highway was completed in 1956, and Big Tujunga Canyon Road in 1958, thus ensuring job security for the rescue team. Increasing mobility led to more car crashes and lost hikers, resulting in a growing number of calls for the rescue team. In 1965 they became the Montrose Search and Rescue Team, as they have been ever since. They were now at the top of their game and nationally recognized, a status they have enjoyed ever since. They are still volunteers, but they receive professional training. They go to the Sheriff Academy and become badged reserve officers, become certified EMTs, receive specialized mountain rescue training, all while still doing their day jobs as teachers, store clerks, and insurance salesmen. It's not just for men either, as there have been several women team members over the years, two of them serving as Captains of the team. This team is also a testament to the saying "Old guys rule!" as many team members are, well, "mature." Some are in their 50s and 60s, and a couple are still serving in their 70s. They are on call all day and night, every day of the year, to respond and save human life.

Here is a sampling of the thousands of true stories of heroism, tragedy, and the daily efforts of a few good and generous citizens to save lives. They are true heroes of our community.

All quotes were taken from the historical records kept by the Montrose Search and Rescue Team unless specified otherwise.

In 1947, the rescue team acquired their first rescue vehicle, a jeep pulling a trailer loaded with lots of rope and other equipment. In the early days of mountain rescue, it was all about ropes and pulleys, as powered winches and helicopters were unavailable to the team.

In 1957, the Sheriff Emergency Reserve Team poses for a group shot on the Angeles Crest Highway. Note the Western-style vests.

By 1960, the team had moved to completely white uniforms, somewhat impractical for men hiking the backcountry of the San Gabriel Mountains. They proudly display their rather unique rescue litter mounted on a bicycle wheel.

In 1961, the white coveralls were accented with web utility belts, and helmet-mounted lights. They now have three Honda trail bikes to help with back-country patrols.

The History of the Montrose Search and Rescue Team—Our Local Heroes

In 1962, they went for a Sheriff uniform shirt above the still impractical white pants.

By the '80s and '90s, the Montrose Search and Rescue team (their name since 1965) had settled into a version of the practical outfits they wear today.

As the Angeles Crest Highway opened up, the casualties mounted in car-over-the-side crashes, many involving alcohol.

Early rescues of victims of car over-the-side crashes were admittedly crude, hand-lowering a man down by a rope.

As time went on, the rescues still involved rope, but powered winches did the lifting.

Above: Soon helicopters joined the team, and injured parties could be flown quickly to hospitals. Here a rescue helicopter has just delivered a victim to the landing pad at Verdugo Hills Hospital.

Left: An experienced member of the team instructs a new recruit, literally showing him the ropes.

Mountain Rescues

THE BOY WHO MISSED THE BUS

In February of 1958, 100 elementary school-age inner-city kids from South-Central LA boarded busses of the Catholic Youth Organization (CYO) for a trip to the snow. For many of these kids, this would be their first time in the snow; for others, their first time in the mountains. They were excited as they wound up Angeles Crest Highway, reaching Chilao Flats just in time for lunch. After eating, and some exuberant play, roll-call was taken as the kids re-boarded the buses to head to the snow at Mt. Waterman a few miles away. Lots of snow-play, another roll-call to re-board, and at dusk the buses returned to South-Central. Panic ensued when they came up one kid short, every youth-worker's nightmare. Ten-year-old Robert Douglas was missing. Another boy revealed he had playfully answered for Robert at both roll calls. The Sheriffs were called, but the CYO didn't know if Robert had been left at Chilao or Waterman. By morning the Montrose Search and Rescue Team (MSR) and the Sheriff's Posse (a unit of horse-mounted Deputies) were at both locations.

    Robert had actually gotten separated from the group at the first stop, Chilao Flats. After finishing his lunch, he saw some flowers nearby. Hoping to pick a bouquet for his mom, the boy followed a trail of wildflowers, picking as he went. He hadn't been paying attention to his surroundings and he suddenly realized he was completely alone. Robert was terrified and tried to backtrack. When he realized he was truly lost, he remembered hearing someone say if lost, follow a stream. There was a stream there, which he followed in the wrong direction, upstream, taking him away from Chilao. All night the boy walked along the slippery, icy stream. He cried and prayed and was terribly cold as the temperature dipped below freezing. The next day Robert saw a helicopter twice, but he was in too dense foliage to be seen. Another cold, desperate night was spent alone and shivering. The next day found him stumbling on his numb legs along the increasingly steepening creek-side. He finally crept out on a steep ledge above the stream and was trapped.

    The search was in full swing at both Waterman and Chilao, where fifty searchers fanned out. SAR teams from both Montrose and Altadena, Sheriff Deputies, CYO workers and even Robert's older brother were backed up by a Sheriff helicopter that buzzed the steep terrain. The weather was deteriorating, getting colder with rising wind, and snow in the forecast. As the second day

Above: A lost hiker is treated for exhaustion after being found by the Montrose Search and Rescue team.

Left: Team members often search through the night, hiking miles of back-country trails in the dark.

turned to night the searchers were getting grim. Complicating matters, another rescue nearby was tightening resources.

Just as the sun was setting for the third night, a CYO worker, glassing with binoculars, spotted the boy far off on a cliff side. He radioed in and search teams converged on his approximate location in the dark. Four hours later (after rescuing some other CYO workers trapped on a ledge), they heard the faint cries of the boy in the darkness.

It was too dark to take Robert off the slippery ledge, so the thirteen rescuers bundled the hungry, exhausted boy in blankets, fed him his first food in two days, and built a roaring fire. They settled in for the night in the freezing weather. In the morning, the rescue copter came in and spotted a likely landing spot some distance from the rescue party. The copter roped a deputy with an axe down to the landing zone, and he cleared the area of trees and bushes so the copter could land safely. The MSR team carried the boy down from the ledge, as his legs and hands were swollen and useless from frostbite. Despite his exhaustion, Robert grinned ear-to-ear as he was loaded into the rescue chopper for his first helicopter ride.

He was taken to a Glendale hospital where his frostbitten legs were saved after six days of work by doctors. One of the doctors remarked on the boy's ordeal, "It's hard to believe a human body could endure such torture." Another successful rescue by the Montrose Search and Rescue.

KIDS HIKE TO MT. LUKENS TURNS DEADLY

On a warm and clear winter morning, December 30, 1971, the neighborhood kids from the 3200 block of Henrietta Avenue decided to hike to Mt. Lukens to visit the freshly fallen snow. They had all done the hike many times before, being so close to the mountains, and their parents knew where they were going. The trailhead was just a couple of blocks away in Dunsmore Canyon, today's Deukmejian Park. Fifteen-year-old Barbara led the group consisting of her brother Ed, twelve, along with others from the neighborhood: Dan, twelve, Chris, eleven, and Timmy, eleven. With temperatures in the 70s, they wore only jeans, jackets, and light tennis shoes.

It was one of those glorious sunny days for hiking, and they passed many other hikers on the trails. They made the summit easily by noon where they stopped to eat a lunch they had brought. At the top of Mt. Lukens, the weather was completely different. Icy cold wind roared, and the snow at the top was unexpectedly deep, waist-high in spots. It was suddenly too cold for what they were wearing. They needed to get out of the snow quickly. Two teenage boys they met at the top told them that if they needed to get warm, they should go down the Haines Canyon Road towards Tujunga. They said it would get them out of the snow faster.

They took that route, but the snow didn't end. They walked on and on, pushing their cold feet through the snow. The wind picked up and was blowing snow from the drifts into their faces. They were getting tired now and their feet were completely numb. The sun was going down. Barbara and her brother at some point realized they were no longer wearing shoes, that they had been pulled off their lifeless feet by the deep snow. Timmy, the smallest of the group was getting too tired to go further. Barbara tried to carry him, but on her shoeless, numb feet but she didn't get far. As darkness fell, they could see the lights of the Crescenta Valley below, even pick out their own neighborhood. They decided as a group that one of them had to try to go ahead and get help, so Danny struck out alone. Barbara described what happened next:

At first, we were alright—then I noticed that Timmy was getting sleepy. I had read that you mustn't fall asleep in the snow, that you never wake up. I told everyone that we had to keep awake, not to go to sleep, so we poked each other and talked. Timmy couldn't feel the cold after a while and he started to talk to himself. I shouted at him, trying to keep him awake. The wind was so strong that we couldn't hear each other above its roar. We had stopped behind a large bush. I hoped it would keep the wind off, but it didn't work.

All of a sudden, I noticed that Timmy wasn't talking anymore, he was just staring. Chris tried to listen to his heart and he didn't hear anything. I tried to give him mouth-to-mouth resuscitation. We also hit him on the chest to get his heart going again.

Then I just thought, he's probably dead. For a while we just sat there looking at him. It was like a nightmare. We didn't think it was real. We got terribly frightened. I decided we couldn't stay there any longer or the same thing would happen to us. So we got up and again tried to get down below the snow level. I just knew that we had to do something.

What had been a short hike, literally within sight of their homes, had now turned into a deadly fight for their lives. The trio only made it a short distance before the wind became so strong they couldn't stand upright. They were being knocked down by the wind gusts. Barbara accidently dropped her canteen over the side of the mountain, tried to retrieve it, but gave up. The kids found a small outcrop that gave them a little shelter from the icy wind. There they huddled and began to fade from consciousness.

Danny hiked the four or five miles through dark in the cold, screaming wind, and came out on Haines Canyon Boulevard. He hitched a ride back home from a resident. At 9 p.m. he burst into his house where the worried parents of the group of kids had gathered. "They're stuck, you've got to help them," he stammered from frozen lips. The Montrose Search and Rescue Team was called out to find the four kids.

The team had just spent the entire previous night searching the cold mountains above Altadena for some kids who had, unknown to their parents, merely spent the night at a friend's house. They were bone tired. But the team responded to this new call, as they always do. They stopped first at the house where Danny was, interviewed him, then put him in the rescue truck. Under Danny's directions they drove up the Haines Canyon fire road. When the team picked up Danny's footprints in the snow, they drove the exhausted boy back home, while the team continued on foot.

The icy cold wind was screaming. The strongest gusts were actually knocking the team members to their knees. They tracked Danny's trail for several miles, then spotted tracks seeming to go over the side. (This was where Barbara had dropped the canteen over the edge.) Team member Dan Hensley stepped to the edge of the road overlooking the valley to radio this info in. He was startled when he heard what sounded like a single bark of a dog, distinct over the howling wind. He spun around, playing his flashlight over the snow. Out of the corner of his eye, he saw what appeared to be three tree stumps sticking up out of the snow. But when Hensley shown his light on them, he saw that it was the kids. They were flocked white with snow, completely still and silent, and staring straight at him. The sight scared the hell out of Hensley, as they looked dead.

He rushed to them, and found they were alive, although barely. As he and the other team members wrapped them in blankets, Hensley made a quick medical assessment. They were all barely coherent, somewhat delirious. But the oldest girl Barbara's feet were in very bad shape. She had lost her shoes walking in the snow and was now barefoot. Her feet were black and hard. Hensley sat facing her and put her feet against his bare stomach while he tried to massage them. They were like two cold blocks of steel against his skin. At 3 a.m. they carried the kids down the mountain, while other team members went 300 yards further up and retrieved Timmy's body.

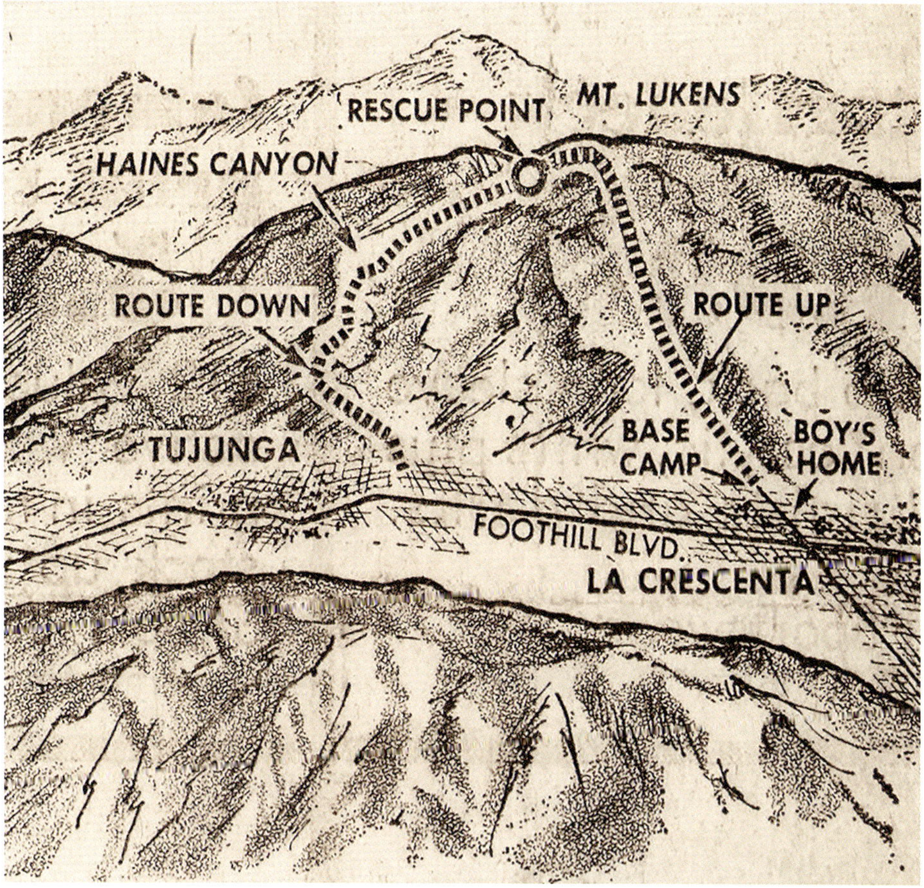

![Map showing Mt. Lukens, Rescue Point, Haines Canyon, Route Down, Route Up, Tujunga, Base Camp, Boy's Home, Foothill Blvd., La Crescenta]

Above: This map was published in a newspaper at the time, showing the route the group of kids took, and where they were rescued.

Right: As one of the rescued children is wheeled into the hospital, a tearful mother embraces him.

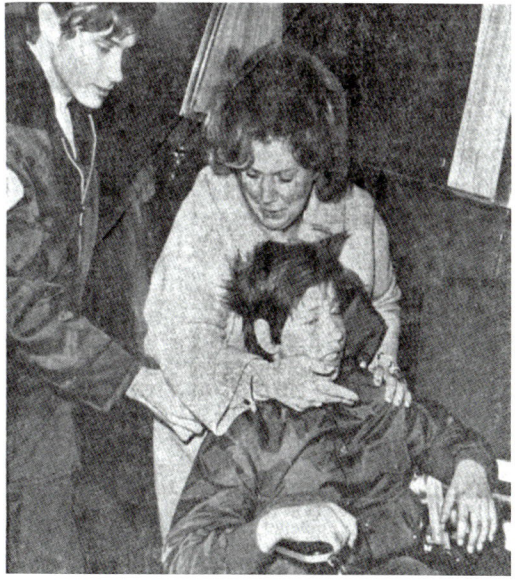

Above left: Barbara's friends brought her a big toy turtle to raise her spirits. Due to her positive experience in the hospital, Barbara later became a nurse.

Above right: Barbara smiles at the hospital, feeling lucky to be alive. Her feet are still heavily bandaged.

The two younger boys were treated for hypothermia and released, but Barbara's feet were in danger of amputation. After several weeks in the hospital Barbara was released, feet intact. The doctors attributed this to Hensley's quick action on massaging her feet. Interestingly she later went on to become a nurse. The community mourned Timmy's death, and the Montrose Search and Rescue Team spent time talking to kids at Valley View Elementary, where Timmy had been a student. And in a Hollywood style ending, Barbara's older sister Sue was so grateful for her sister's rescue that she later joined the MSR team herself. She served with them for many, many years, giving back to the team that had saved her sister's life.

HELPING TO SOLVE THE MURDER OF A BEAUTIFUL MODEL

Besides the rescues that the Montrose Search and Rescue Team (MSR) performs on a regular basis, they occasionally do some detective work as well. Such was the case for longtime MSR team member Fred Koegler way back in the fall of 1995, in the case of the disappearance and murder of Linda Sobek. It was a famous case, big in the news at the time, and it was Koegler who located her body.

In November of 1995, professional photographer Charles Rathbun was assigned to do some glamour shots of a new Lexus model for an auto magazine. He contacted twenty-seven-year-old model Linda Sobek to accompany him on the shoot and to pose in the photos. To make a long and gruesome story short, after sexually assaulting her, he strangled her to death and buried her body in a shallow grave on a lonely dirt road far back in the Angeles Forest.

Her disappearance was a mystery for a few days, since she hadn't told anyone where she was going the day of her murder. The first break on the case came when a Forest Service worker emptying a trashcan on Angeles Crest Highway just above La Canada found some professional photos of a beautiful girl. He took them home, and then was horrified when he saw they matched the broadcast images of the missing model. He called the police, who now had a possible location.

The MSR team was called out to begin searching the roads and backroads of the Angeles Forest. They examined every turnout, and every place that a car could have gone over the side. In the meantime, the police had found more of Linda Sobek's possessions in that same trashcan, along with some paperwork with Charles Rathbun's name on it. Rathbun was located and brought by helicopter to the Mill Creek Ranger Station, which had been set up as a command center. Fred Koegler and Al McGee were patrolling the dirt roads near Pacifico Mountain. They just happened to check back in at the Ranger Station when Rathbun was flown in.

Rathbun was at that point a mess, feigning remorse, and telling the authorities he had accidently run over the model while demonstrating some driving maneuvers. Koegler approached the helicopter, where he was able to overhear Rathbun describing to deputies in vague terms where he had buried Sobek. Koegler recognized the landmarks Rathbun described, so he and McGee drove to a lonely backroad turnout. There they saw the arm of the buried murder victim sticking out of her shallow grave. They taped off the scene and called in the authorities. Thanks to the work of Koegler and McGee, police now had a body, and Rathbun's story began to unravel. After a sensational trial, Rathbun was convicted of murder and sentenced to life in prison without the possibility of parole.

Since Fred Koegler had such a large part in solving of the case, he was called to testify in the trial. Rathbun's defense attorney was particularly interested in the way that Koegler had found the body, probably with the intention of saying the body would not have been located were it

Left: The pretty blonde model Linda Sobek was also a cheerleader for a professional football team.

Below: A distraught Charles Rathbun sits in a Sheriff helicopter at Mill Creek Ranger station, trying to describe where he had buried Sobek's body.

Photographer Charles Rathbun, convicted of murder, looks appropriately evil in this courtroom photo.

not for his client's cooperation. Koegler's testimony countered that assertion. Before he had overheard Rathbun's descriptions, he had already gotten tire prints from the murder vehicle and was preparing to use them to track the vehicle on the dirt roads. He told the court he was ninety percent sure that he or another MSR team member would have found the grave, based on the MSR's tracking abilities.

The MSR team is well trained in backcountry tracking. They received special training by the US Border Patrol in tracking border-crossers across the desert. They regularly compete in tracking competitions with other search and rescue teams from across Southern California, and often win the competitions.

Fred Koegler received a commendation for his work on this case. Now in his seventies, he is still an active member of the Montrose Search and Rescue Team.

WACKED OUT IN THE WOODS, OR THE GIRL WHO PARTIED TOO HARD

In September of 1993, a nineteen-year-old girl from Tujunga met some friends at the top of Mt. Wilson for some serious partying. In the dark of night, she parked her car near the radio towers, and walked down through the trees to where her friends were. Sometime that night, the girl, apparently dazed and confused, wandered off from the group. She stumbled around in the dark completely lost, falling down several times, and slowly heading downhill. It's unclear what was going on in the girl's head, as she continued stumbling down the hill, eventually coming across a stream, the very steep Eaton Canyon Creek.

After a couple of days, she was reported missing, and her car was located. A search by the MSR, along with the Altadena and Sierra Madre teams was organized, but the girl was off trail, down in canyons and very hard to spot. After the girl had been missing for an entire seven days, she was finally spotted by some hikers.

A young married couple, Andreas and Katie of Pasadena had decided on an early morning hike to Eaton Canyon Falls from another parallel trail, cutting cross-country following a ridgeline. They traversed the ridge, hit the creek, and began to follow it down to the falls. As they rounded a bend in the stream they were confronted with a bizarre sight. Andreas said, "All of the sudden we round this one bend and there is this apparition!" The lost girl was completely naked, but so dirt-soaked that she literally "matched the landscape." The young couple gave her some of their clothes and some candy they had in their pockets.

The lost girl was shaky but able to tell her strange story to the couple. She told them she had been partying with friends, had wandered off, and had been crawling down the creek bed for days. She had lost her clothes and shoes three or four days previous. The stream is extremely steep, with several unclimbable waterfalls, and she described how she threw rocks off the top to make sure the water below was deep enough, then leaped over the edge into the pool below. She described falling several times, being disoriented and even unconscious. She had no food the entire week and she had traveled about ten miles.

Andreas carried the girl uphill to a clearing where rescue teams would be able to see her. Leaving his wife Katie with the girl, Andreas scrambled quickly back the way he had come, at one point accidentally sliding off the ridge into some cactus below. He found the authorities, and a helicopter was dispatched to his described clearing.

Unfortunately, Los Angeles County had been going through some ill-timed budget cuts at that time, and the MSR's big rescue chopper had been grounded. A smaller Fire Department helicopter tried to pull the lost girl off the clearing, but their winch wasn't long enough to reach her. After several hours of waiting another larger chopper was pressed into service and the lost girl was winched up. She was flown to a hospital where she was treated for dehydration, scrapes, bruises and a broken wrist—not bad considering her ordeal—a very lucky girl.

The reason for her walk in the woods was unclear. The girl was too disoriented to answer questions from Deputies just after her rescue. A hospital spokesman said the girl told them she had gone off on her own to think. Whatever the reason, she had made an amazing journey: seven days outdoors, traveling down the face of a sheer mountainside, no trail, no food, half the trip done naked and with no shoes. When found, she was very nearly all the way down the mountain. An epic journey worthy of a novel—if only she could remember it!

Andreas and his wife were philosophical about their part in the rescue. Andreas said, "Somehow Katie and I were called to get up that morning and go hiking. It was very spiritual."

SAVING NEARLY 600 PEOPLE TRAPPED ON MT. WILSON

It was a gorgeous Easter Sunday in April of 1965. Snow covered the San Gabriel Mountains, but the springtime sun pushed the temperatures into the 70s. Scores of motorists made the drive up Angeles Crest Highway, turning on to the narrow twisting road to Mt. Wilson that skirts the sheer mountainside. Each car picked its way around a few rocks that had fallen onto the pavement, loosened by the quickly melting snow, but no one thought much of it.

After a few hours at the summit, cars began to descend the steep roadway. At 2:30 p.m., a group of about twenty-five cars approached the area where a few rocks had fallen earlier, a couple of miles above Angeles Crest Highway. A witness described what happened next: "I saw the first big boulder hit the roadway and bounce into the canyon. Then it looked like the whole mountain was coming down." A car in the lead was hit by a huge rock which landed on its hood, stalling the car. The occupants got out and pushed the car forward as more rocks came down behind it. A passenger in one of the following cars said, "It started with a rumble. Then it sounded like an explosion!" Tons of mud, snow and debris slid onto the roadway and spilled down into the canyon. Boulders as big as cars were mixed in. The road was completely blocked for 100 feet or more. Trapped behind the slide were approximately 100 cars, and nearly 600 people. Amazingly no one had been injured.

Sheriffs and the Montrose Search and Rescue responded and gave the trapped crowd some tough alternatives. They could wait in their cars for however many hours it took to clear the road, or they could abandon their cars and pick their way across the landslide escorted by the MSR members. All but a handful chose the latter.

Walking across the unstable landslide proved too risky, and a few rocks were still falling. But the rock wall guardrail at the edge of the road was still intact. The top of the rock wall was cleared of debris and the MSR strung a guide rope three feet above the wall. The trick now was going to be helping nearly 600 people walk what amounted to a 100-foot-long tightrope. Imagine walking on the one-foot-wide rough surfaced rock wall with just a single rope to hang onto. It's now dark. On one side is a shifting pile of boulders you just watched crash down, and on the other is a straight drop of 500 feet or more into blackness.

Ten Deputies walked the wall first to show the crowd how to do it, and the people waiting behind gingerly stepped up onto the wall to follow. One said later, "Most of the people were calm, but some were panicky. One woman said she almost fainted." MSR members and deputies walked with the more fearful. "Don't look down" they told the walkers over and over. One woman said she couldn't help looking. "The walkway was so narrow. I would have fallen, but a deputy grabbed me." Children had to be carried, leaving the carrier off-balance, and without hands to hold the guide-rope.

After several hours the entire crowd had been brought across the landslide, where several warm Sheriff Department busses waited. As soon as everyone was across, road crews set up floodlights and began clearing the slide. Nine busloads of the trapped motorists were brought down the Angeles Crest Highway to La Crescenta. On duty at the American Legion Hall to receive them was the Crescenta-Canada Emergency Corps (the equivalent of today's CERT team—we've always been a community of volunteers). They'd set up a phone bank, food and hot coffee, and had rallied a fleet of taxis to take the weary home. It had been a thrilling and amazing night for both the rescuers and the rescuees. One tired mom said, "It was our first trip here, and our last!" Not completely accurate. Unfortunately, she'd have to return to Mt. Wilson one more time to get her trapped car.

HIKERS BIT OFF MORE THAN THEY COULD CHEW

It's a common mistake. Hikers read about a particular hike, check their maps, think that it looks pretty easy, and head out for what they estimate will be a day trip. But they're halfway through the hike and it's getting dark and cold.

Such was the case for eight adult hikers in summer of 1990. They intended to rappel down a series of twelve waterfalls along Fox Creek, just below Mount Gleason in the Angeles Forest. It was a full day of hiking, but all eight hikers were confident they could make it from their starting point to a pickup spot where someone's wife waited with a van. When they didn't show up at the end of the day and darkness fell, the MSR was called.

Here's where the team's preplanning was put to use. Before starting out, they met with the woman who was to pick up the group. She knew their starting point and their intended destination, so the team had a good idea of the search area. She was also able to tell them the

The rock wall with the rope strung above it. A young man looks back after having just crossed over on the narrow wall. On one side is rubble, on the other is a black void.

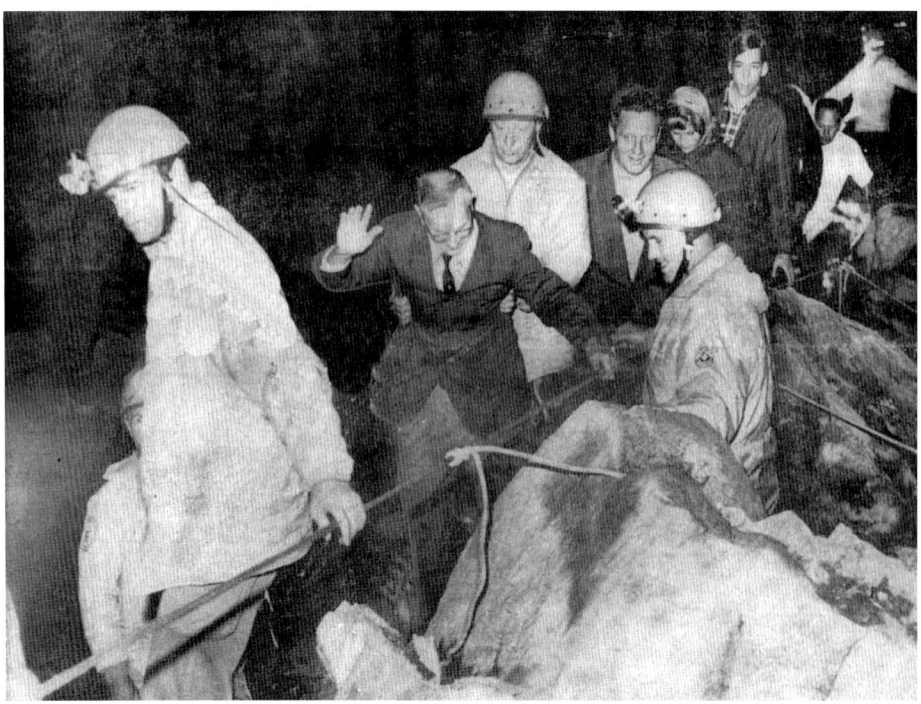

Montrose Search and Rescue team members carefully guide the trapped motorists along the narrow rock wall.

Right: One of the many high waterfalls. Imagine attempting to rappel down this in the dark.

Below: The team trains hard for scenarios just like this. Here they winch a victim from another rescue up a sheer waterfall.

equipment the lost hikers had with them. The team now knew that the hikers, although they had some backcountry training, were not clothed properly, didn't have enough food, and the ropes they had were inadequate for rappelling. Reviewing maps, the team found a remote fire road that would put them very close to the first waterfall, trimming off about six hours of hiking.

After midnight, the search began. They quickly found the lost hikers' fresh footprints headed downstream, so they knew they were on the right track. The team easily rappelled down the first waterfall, about eighty feet of slippery rock face. They reached the next waterfall, a little steeper, and quickly rappelled it as well. The descent of the second waterfall ended in a chest-deep pool, so they knew the lost hikers would be wet, increasing the chances of hypothermia.

The team continued following footprints downstream to the top of the third waterfall, and that's where they found the eight hikers. They were cold, wet and exhausted, but really happy to see the rescue team. None of the hikers were injured and it was still dark, so the rescue team passed out blankets and granola bars and kindled a campfire to wait out the night in relative comfort. At daybreak, the team rallied the hikers, and continued downstream looking for a spot their rescue helicopter could put down. The rescue team and the hikers descended four more waterfalls, this time with proper equipment and techniques. Just before noon they finally found a clearing for the chopper, and everyone was lifted out.

The team often deals in tragedy, but this event had a happy ending. Because the team researched the rescue before heading off, they were able to reach the hikers before hypothermia took its toll, and before the hikers attempted to continue downstream. The hikers were grateful for the swift response. They had simply underestimated the time needed for the hike, and they were indeed beginning to worry about hypothermia. In the words of one of the rescuers, "they had simply bit off more than they could chew." The grateful hikers afterward sent a care package to the MSR made up of the types of supplies the team had used in their rescue.

The MSR relies on extensive training to carry them successfully through rescues such as this one. They spend literally hundreds of hours each year training in mountaineering, reading terrain, and keeping themselves in peak physical condition. Rope work such as they used in this rescue is part of their basic training. They have all the skills of first responders for first aid, stabilizing injuries, and knowledge of disease and trauma. They are also trained in how to think like a lost hiker, and how to keep people from panicking under stress.

They do all of this as volunteers. They receive a token one dollar a year. Their real pay comes in the form of the satisfaction of saving lives and giving back to our community.

SADLY, SOMETIMES IT'S JUST BODY RETRIEVAL

The Montrose Search and Rescue's job is usually just what their name implies, both search and rescue. But often they are sent in knowing the people they are after are already dead, and they are simply retrieving the remains. In 1966 at the so-called Loop Fire, that was the case.

On November 1, 1966, drought conditions and blistering 100-degree heat, combined with deadly Santa Ana winds had sparked nearly a dozen wildfires all through Southern California. At dawn, a faulty powerline fell in the San Gabriel Mountains just above Pacoima and had set over 2,000 acres ablaze. An army of firefighters attacked it all day. So-called Hotshot crews were trucked or flown in from several locations, including the elite El Carizo Hotshots, who proudly wore green berets to denote their status as the "best of the best." Hotshot crews do the on-the-ground hand-to-hand fighting of fire control, and the twenty-five El Carizo Hotshots were put high up on the rocky slope of a canyon that had already burned over to mop-up and establish a strong firebreak. It was now late afternoon.

Unbeknownst to the crew, down in the canyon a unique situation had developed. Superheated air had accumulated and compressed. The wind suddenly shifted, pushing oxygen into the hot air, just as a partially burned bush rekindled. Just as blowing on a smoldering ember can cause it to burst into flame, the hot air in the canyon bottom exploded. The crew on the slope above heard a boom, then a noise like a jet engine. The air around their eyes went wavy as the superheated air was pushed upslope past them, followed by roaring sheets of flame. The crew was knocked to the ground by the shockwave, while the air around them rose to 2500 degrees. For about thirty seconds they curled on the ground while the air exploded. The more experienced stuffed handkerchiefs in their mouths to protect their lungs, the less experienced died. The flash fire went out, and a helicopter came in immediately. It balanced one skid on a rock on the steep slope, while the survivors, their skin hanging off in shreds, piled in. They left ten bodies behind.

As darkness fell, the Montrose Search and Rescue hiked up the smoldering canyon to retrieve the ten bodies. La Crescenta insurance agent Warren Boehm had just joined the MSR. He said,

> It was like a scene out of Hell. With the roaring flames to light our way, we found ten charred bodies. They were all within a 100-yard area. One of the dead men had his arms up over his face. It was like he was trying to shield his face. The others were huddled on the ground on their sides with their knees drawn up. It was almost as if they were asleep. It's a night I'll never forget.

Scattered everywhere were the Hotshot's charred helmets, canteens, tools and scraps of clothing dropped in their desperate last moments.

The MSR team checked each body for unlikely signs of life. They had brought hand-held basket rescue stretchers with them. They carefully wrapped each fallen firefighter in plastic, then loaded them onto the stretchers. They carefully carried the stretchers down the smoldering hillside to the canyon floor where the bodies were taken to the morgue. The next day Boehm returned to lead newsmen back up to the site where the bodies had been located. As a result, he ended up on a nearly full front-page Herald Examiner photo, showing him grimly holding a blackened canteen one of the hotshots had dropped.

In the next 2 months, two more of the young El Cariso Hotshots died from their burns, while the rest of the crew went through years of healing. El Cariso Park in Sylmar, just below the area where the deaths had occurred, was created as a memorial to the fallen El Cariso Hot Shots, and a monument was erected in the park. In 2016, the survivors gathered at the park for a tearful fiftieth anniversary of the tragedy. The Montrose Search and Rescue Team will always remember that night, the night they retrieved the bodies of those brave firefighters.

Above: The survivors and their families pose in front of the plaque at El Cariso Park at the Fiftieth Anniversary Ceremony.

Opposite above: The MSR team carries the burned bodies of the firefighters out to waiting helicopters.

Opposite below: The day after the disaster, a sad Warren Boehm holds up a charred canteen dropped by one of the fallen Hotshots as they tried to escape.

LOST WOMEN HIKERS KEPT THEIR WITS

Longtime friends Nancy and Vicki were young, just out of their teens, when they planned an overly ambitious hike one Saturday in January 1988. Their day hike was to be from Trail Canyon in Big Tujunga to the top of Condor Peak, looping back to Vogel Flats, a round trip of about fourteen miles. It had been raining but was clearing when they embarked. They wore sweatshirts and rain ponchos and carried food and water. But they were not prepared for the condition of the trail. It started off well-marked, but as they went higher the trail began to peter out into a rough track, and the climbing got more difficult.

By the time they reached the summit of Condor Peak, it was 4 p.m. and they were bone tired, legs beginning to cramp. They lost the trail entirely at this point. A heavy wet fog moved in, further confusing their sense of direction. They feared that they would have to spend the night, and they steeled their resolve. As darkness fell, so did their spirits, and a battle with their emotions began. They were tired, damp, and cold, and depression, anger, and frustration crept into their minds. There was a gnawing fear that they would never find their way out. But they fought the fear and encouraged each other, kept the fear from turning to panic. Nancy later said, "We were confident of our abilities."

About 7 p.m. they found a stream and began to follow it downhill. They finally stopped when they reached a waterfall that disappeared into darkness. It started to rain. Wet and cold, they lay down between two boulders with their ponchos stretched over as a tarp. Sleep came only intermittently. Between bouts of shivering, Vicki kept her spirits up by telling herself jokes and making up funny TV commercials in her head.

Fortunately, the two women had performed the most important safety task of any hike—they told someone where they would be hiking. At 7 p.m. Saturday night, Vicki's dad called them in as missing, and by 8 p.m., twenty-three members of Montrose Search and Rescue Team were on their trail. From Trail Canyon, they tracked the women's footprints all the way to the top of Condor Peak. But, on the rocky top they lost the trail. The MSR split up into smaller groups, some to search all night, others to get some sleep so they could renew the search in the morning. That night in the dark, one search party came within half a mile of the women, but fog and rain kept the women from seeing their lights or hearing their whistles.

Sunday morning dawned to a cold fog and rain. Nancy and Vicki climbed down around the waterfall, one of many they would face, and continued downstream. They pushed their failing bodies all day and kept their minds focused on a positive outcome. By late afternoon Sunday they hit Big Tujunga Canyon Road and were picked up by a Sheriff patrol car.

At 4 p.m. Sunday, the radio call went out that the lost hikers had been found, and the scattered MSR teams headed down the mountain. Ironically, one three-man group got hung up in the dark at a 100-foot waterfall, perhaps the same one that had stopped the women the night before. Erring on the side of safety they radioed for help getting down, and the other members of the team returned up the mountain for them. One of the trapped men later said, "The team

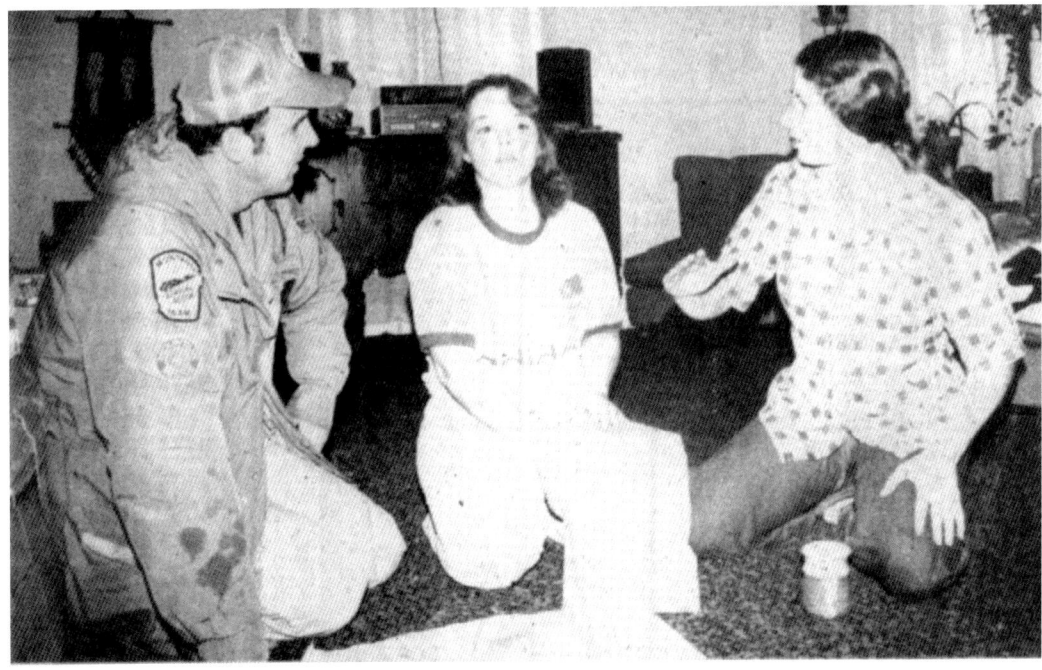

After their adventure, Nancy and Vicki discuss what happened with a Montrose Search and Rescue team member.

had been out all Saturday night and all-day Sunday. But when they found out we were stuck, they all came back. It's a group, and I can't tell you how enjoyable it has been for me to be a member."

After the search, an MSR leader said the only mistake the women had made was to press on after they knew they were lost. "Don't wander. That's where the danger comes in." Indeed, had they stopped at Condor Peak, they would have been found on Saturday night. The women had been lucky, but keeping a positive attitude also paid off. They had kept going by mental strength. Nancy reflected later "It really is interesting what strength can come from the mind."

BUSY THANKSGIVING WEEKEND

The pressure on the Montrose Search and Rescue Team increases on holiday weekends. This account of two rescues on Sunday of the Thanksgiving weekend in 1986 shows how this brave rescue team often sacrifices their holidays to save lives.

At the same moment that particular Sunday, two different groups of forest visitors had joined the hundreds of LA residents enjoying perfect weather in the mountains. One of them was a young family with a baby out for a pleasant drive through the gorgeous San Gabriel Mountains, while the other was a group of novice hikers, sporting ambitious plans mixed with poor preparation. In both cases the MSR would save lives.

Two MSR members on patrol that day were parked at Clear Creek Vista, when a car screeched up. The young couple inside screamed that their baby had stopped breathing. The officers checked the nine-month-old boy, who the parents said had inexplicably stopped breathing just two minutes earlier. One of the two MSR members said later:

> I don't know why he wasn't breathing, but he was blue. I tilted his neck and checked to see if anything was lodged in there, and then I administered mouth-to-mouth resuscitation. The color started to return. We were worried. It was critical for the baby because he hadn't been breathing for two minutes. After six minutes you start to get brain damage, and we were fifteen minutes from help.

They transferred the child to the rescue truck and took off down Angeles Crest Highway at high speed while performing CPR. In less than a minute the baby started breathing again, crying in fact, and they met an ambulance at the base of the hill for the trip to Verdugo Hills Hospital. In the craziness of the rescue, they never even got the parent's names, although they did get tearful thank-yous from the young couple. The MSR team member said, "We've handled a lot of car and motorcycle accidents, but we never handled a baby who was not breathing. We were really happy he was alright."

While this was happening, a group of four inexperienced hikers were climbing the trail to the top of Strawberry Peak. They had parked a car at Red Box where they had started and another at Colby Canyon where they planned to come out. However, as they reached the top of Strawberry Peak the trail began to peter out, and they were unsure of where to go. There they met other hikers, who inadvertently sent them the wrong direction. After a while they realized they were not headed toward Colby Canyon, so they backtracked, but became disoriented. Night began to fall. They were dressed for a typical perfect fall day in LA: shorts, T-shirts and tennis shoes, so as darkness crept in, they began to get very cold. The wind picked up and the temperatures

A rescued hiker and their MSR rescuer are pulled into the door of the helicopter after being winched up from the ground.

dropped into the 30s. The group had no food, and no warm clothes. The hikers wisely decided to stop wandering. With nothing to start a fire, they huddled together, shivering.

In the meantime, worried relatives called them in as missing. The MSR swung into action at 11 p.m. Ten team members were called out, including the two who had just saved the baby. They broke into five two-man teams and began to walk the major trails near where the hikers were supposed to be. But after an all-night search they found no trace of the lost group. At first light, a rescue helicopter joined the team, scouring the dense brush. At 8:30 Monday morning the four hikers were spotted waving to the chopper on a ridgeline, where they were probably trying to warm up in the morning sunshine. The rescue helicopter picked them up with their cable winch, while the search teams were called in. The grateful but cold and hungry hikers were airlifted to Red Box, where paramedics were waiting. They were exhausted but otherwise unharmed and were released with parting advice from the MSR. "I gave them a lecture on mountain safety and the need to be prepared because of the weather. They seemed to understand." said one MSR member with a smile. "It was very thrilling to find them alive."

WHAT'S IT LIKE TO GET "SEARCHED AND RESCUED"?

Although many stories here are life or death struggles for survival, here's a story of a much less dramatic rescue that took place in the summer of 1990. Dan and Jane Rollins relayed the tail of Dan's rescue by the MSR after a hike gone wrong. These kinds of lost hiker rescues make up the majority of the MSR's activities. I asked Dan what it's like to be rescued. He replied, "It's embarrassing—and exciting."

On July 21, 1990, the Rollins organized a big family picnic in the Switzer picnic area, with the highlight being an adventurous backcountry hike for all the little nieces and nephews. They would hike down the Arroyo to JPL. On the hike would be Dan and his five-year-old son; Dan's sister and her two kids, seven and eight; and a nephew, six. Not going with them on the hike would be a map, accidentally left in the car. But Dan had done the hike before and felt confident. Typical of organizing kids, they got a late start, about 4:30 p.m.

They hiked easily downhill, but slower than Dan had anticipated. Reaching Switzer Falls, they indulged the sweating kids in a swim in the pool below the falls, further delaying their hike. Afterward, Dan took a wrong fork, a common error on this trail. The sun was getting low as they hiked about an hour the wrong direction, up Bear Canyon, which has no outlet. The trail began to peter out, and Dan had the sinking feeling he was lost. It was darkening quickly as they hit the end of the box canyon, so Dan figured they had better give up and stop for the night.

Dan and his sister were careful not to transmit their anxiety to the kids. Actually, they were well set up. Dan and his sister were experienced campers, it was a warm night, and they had water, granola bars and a lighter. Dan lit a campfire, and they settled in for the evening, singing campfire songs, eating granola bars, and generally trying to assure the kids this was all part of the adventure. The kids were having a blast.

Meanwhile back in the parking lot at JPL, Dan's wife Jane was beginning to panic as darkness fell. At 8 p.m. she contacted the ranger, who called out the MSR. They searched the trail through the night, not realizing the group had gone up Bear Canyon. A fearful Jane and her young daughter slept in the car all night, keeping vigil on the trail.

In the morning, Dan and the kids, after a sleepless night, hiked back down Bear Canyon, and rejoined the trail heading back up to Switzer. A small helicopter swept low over the bleary

Dan and son Bobbie pose for another of the seemingly endless news shots after their rescue.

group, and called out to ask if they were lost hikers, and said they would return with the rescue chopper. An hour later, the gigantic rescue helicopter settled into a hover just above the group, turning the trail into a hurricane of blowing dirt and leaves. A man was lowered down, and one at a time, the kids, Dan, and his sister were cabled up to the noisy chopper. A short ride to the JPL parking lot, and as the chopper spun around for a landing, its open door revealed a sea of news vans waiting for the group. Unfortunately for Dan, it had been a slow news day, and Dan and the kids now faced a gauntlet of microphones and cameras. While Dan sheepishly tried to explain his error, the kids joyfully mugged for the cameras and delighted interviewers with kid's-eye-views of their adventure.

The family recorded the multiple broadcasts from the news channels, and created a wonderful homemade documentary, which has been watched at every family gathering since. As well, the Rollins have donated generously to the MSR since then. One last thing: After the rescue, Dan retrieved his map from the car and had the rescuers sign it. Having searched for Dan and family all night, one of them wrote, "In the future, please get lost between 9 a.m. and 5 p.m. We need our sleep!"

A LOST HIKER CALLS FOR HELP ON HIS CELLPHONE—IN 1991!

It's a common scenario: A hiker gets lost, so he whips out his cellphone, looks for a signal, and calls for help. But when this lost hiker used his cellphone in 1991, he was apparently one of the first to have done that. The story begins in November of 1991. Walter, sixty-four years old, was an experienced hiker, and felt no need to bring a map when he embarked on a day hike in the San Gabriel Mountains around Big Tujunga Canyon. He was very familiar with the route he was on. But, he did decide to drop his big new cellphone into his backpack, just in case of a problem.

Walter's problem was of his own making as he took a wrong turn and ended up on a trail he'd not been on before. He had planned for his wife to pick him up at a pre-arranged point, and he decided to use his new cellphone to call her and say he'd be late. But he faced the same problem then as someone in the same situation today would face in the mountains—no signal. After hiking quite some ways he finally found a spot where he could transmit and called his wife at home. Walter told her he wouldn't make the pre-arranged pick-up point, that he was sort of lost, but that he was hopeful he could find a road to follow.

Having none of that, his wife immediately called the Forest Service, who in turn called out the Montrose Search and Rescue Team. Just as the rescue helicopter was taking off, Walter stumbled across the highway, and thumbed a ride to a Ranger Station. From there he used a land-line to call his wife again, and the search was called off.

Not a very exciting rescue story, but what makes it interesting is the use of the cellphone to call for help. It was so unusual back in '91 that it actually rated a big article in the newspaper. A spokesman for the Forest Service told the paper that it was the first time he had ever heard about anyone doing that. He further said that he expected it to happen more and more as the technology took hold. Indeed Walter, regretting his decision to forget his map, told the paper "I don't think a cellular phone will ever replace a map, but I would recommend it. I'm glad I had it with me."

The newspaper talked to a spokesman from PacTel Cellular. (Remember them? After several mergers, they are now Verizon.) He was quite impressed with this event. He told the paper that there were about 500,000 cellphones in use in the five-county area around Los Angeles. He was also quoted as saying that the diminishing size and weight of cellphones would make cellphones a desirable safety addition for future hikers. He said, "You'll find a lot of them are under a pound and they're pushing a half-pound."

Some of those walkie-talkie style early cellphones were really big. According to the internet, those weighed in at about a pound and a half. They were actually called "brick phones." But by 1991, the newer large-style flip-phones had come out, and they indeed weighed in at about half a pound. Phones got even lighter and smaller as time went on, but the trend has reversed itself now, and they are getting bigger again. Newer smart phones weigh just under half a pound.

Of course, today the cellphone is omnipresent, and every hiker has one. Modern cellphones even have a GPS chip that transmits the phone's location. Search and rescue groups like the Montrose Search and Rescue Team have taken advantage of this new technology to aid in their searches for lost hikers.

MODERN CELLPHONE RESCUES

The last story told the tale of one of the first cellphone calls for help by a lost hiker—circa 1991. Current MSR member Steve Goldsworthy writes about the current state of rescue technology in the field of cellphones. Steve is the rescue team's techie. When asked if they used modern cellphone technology in their searches, he said:

> Not only are we into the technology, but we lead the use of cell technologies county-wide. Not just cellphones, but we've used social media to track people down as well.
> We use everything we can find. We have a specially designed text message that we can send to a hiker's cellphone. When he responds, we automatically receive his coordinates from his GPS enabled cell phone. We ping phones (only works if you have both battery and cell service) and we can obtain cell phone records that might show us an area where you were the last time your cell phone communicated to a cell tower.[1]

Steve refers to being able to "ping" cellphones. The MSR can ask the cellphone company to have the hiker's phone automatically send out a signal (ping). They can then triangulate his location from the cell towers that received the ping. As well, many phones contain tracking software, designed to find lost or stolen phones, which can in turn find the lost hiker holding the phone. A 911 call will also transmit the caller's location.

Steve has passed along a couple of rescue stories that illustrate just how using modern technology has saved lives.

> On September 09, 2014, fresh snow blanketed Mt. Baden-Powell, so two snowboarders and one golden retriever decided to hit the slopes. After a few hours, a new storm was blowing in. The dog fell down a ravine onto a small ledge and became trapped. Darkness was falling and so was visibility. The pet owner jumped down after his dog and then soon realized that he too, was now trapped on a narrow ledge, unable to climb down, or back up. His partner left for help as the storm hit. A 911 call was received at the Palmdale Station. It was the trapped snowboarder, now stuck on the ledge in the dark, with snow falling and blizzard like conditions.
> Rescuers from Antelope Valley SAR responded and after a few hours searching in the cold snowstorm they called Montrose SAR asking for assistance. Search teams were in the field for hours but no sign of the snowboarder was found. We could call him on his cell phone, but we just couldn't find him.
> Around 11 p.m. that night, a Montrose SAR member called him on his cell. The lost snowboarder was now losing all hope of being found. His battery life was at four percent, he was hypothermic, and sounded lethargic and scared on the phone. He said he knew he was going to die soon, and he didn't want to die and leave his dog alone. Nothing seemed to work, and the coordinates we were being given from the 911 system didn't match the area we were told he was in.
> Trying another tack, we asked the victim to take a photo with his cellphone and send it to us. We ran that photo through our computer, and luckily, it was geotagged with his exact location! [Geotagging is when your phone knows your location and adds that location into the properties of your photos.] Quickly those coordinates were converted and a field team dispatched. Less than ten minutes later rescuers were calling his name when they heard his faint reply. Within

"Where am I?!" Sometimes a photo like this can tell the Montrose Search and Rescue team exactly where you are.

the hour they were on the ledge with him and his dog, both of which made it out just fine. The photo that he took of a tree with snow swirling around still resides on our team's computer.[2]

Steve's story shows just how tech-savvy rescuers are using technology to save lives. Next, a story on finding a lost hiker via Facebook.

INJURED MAN FOUND VIA CELLPHONE APP AND FACEBOOK

Continuing with the "cellphone rescues" theme, we get another good story from the Montrose Search and Rescue's technical expert Steve Goldsworthy. Steve has related that today they use every available technology to find lost hikers. Steve tells the story of using Facebook and a fitness tracking software to find an injured bicyclist:

> On June 17, 2011 around 3 p.m., two friends left for a quick mountain bike ride, figuring it would only take a little over two hours to complete. Around 9 p.m., a short 911 cellphone call was received at the Crescenta Valley Sheriff Station. 'My friend fell, he hit his head, I don't know where we are, but we are near a waterfall and my battery is dying ... click ...' The phone was in fact, now dead.
>
> The Montrose SAR team responded, but with very little to go on, including even a place to start looking. The Angeles National Forest is a big place, over 1,000 square miles, with a lot of waterfalls, even in June. All we had was the cell phone number he had used to call us on. After a few required documents between us and the cell company we had his name and address, a resident of Rosemead. Rosemead PD did a door knock, and the girlfriend, now very concerned

about her almost eight-hour overdue boyfriend, answered. We learned that the biker used an app on his cell phone that allowed others to see his ride map. The app was called EndoMondo and it was tied into his Facebook account. A quick log into Facebook and we soon found his ride map, but there were not any latitude or longitudes listed, just a squiggly line of the trail that he had been riding, and for how long. One of our team members recognized those squiggles as the trail over to Ladybug Canyon, then down the Gabrielino trail into Switzers and down into the Arroyo Seco.

By matching that squiggly line up against a Google Earth picture on our monitor, we were able to identify the exact location where his cell phone stopped updating his ride map, which matched the same time that the 911 call was placed. Now we had his exact coordinates at the time of his call. It wasn't long before rescue team members reached him and his riding partner, who indeed had suffered a head injury. Due to heavy fog, a rescue helicopter could not make it to the scene, so the team stayed with them until morning when they were successfully airlifted out. And the nearby waterfall? That turned out to be the Paul Little debris check dam.[3]

That's an amazing piece of detective work on the MSR's part! Steve has some basic cellphone advice for hikers to follow when headed off to the wilderness:

Turn off your cell or place it in airplane mode when in the mountains to help conserve your battery. Turning off apps, wi-fi and GPS can also extend your battery life.

If you encounter an emergency, call 911. Even if it does not appear that you have a signal, make an attempt and let it try to connect for at least twenty seconds. Then move four or five feet and try it again. If your carrier is not available but another competing compatible carrier tower is, the phone will connect an emergency 911 call via the competing carrier.

If calls don't work, try sending a text to someone you trust telling them where you are and what's wrong, and ask them to call 911 for you. Text messages are small packets of data, and you only have to connect to a cell tower for a second or two for them to transmit.

Remember, always have a hiking plan, tell someone your plan, and write it down. MSR has a sample you can use at http://file.lacounty.gov/lasd/cms1_163961.pdf or just search for "LASD hiking plan."

Follow these pieces of advice, and just maybe you won't end up in volume two of this book.

"MAN IN THE WATER!"

There is a memorial at the CV Sheriff station, bearing the names of Sheriff Deputies from that station that have given their lives in the service of their community. One of the names there is that of Reserve Deputy Charles Rea, a member of the famous all-volunteer Montrose Search and Rescue Team.

In the winter of 1969, Los Angeles was in the grip of the fabled "100-year flood." The mountain communities were the hardest hit, as over fifty inches of rain poured down on the San Gabriels, turning every creek into whitewater rapids. The raging river in Big Tujunga Canyon had spread across the entire canyon floor, and the reservoir behind Big Tujunga Dam was full of debris from further upstream. Water and logs, plus big sections of dredging equipment from work being done at the reservoir itself were coming over the top of the dam and were blasting down the canyon. As bridges and roads washed away, the Montrose Search and Rescue Team patrolled the canyon, helping with evacuations and checking the safety of those choosing to stay behind.

On January 26 the team got the call to the Big Tujunga Ranger Station where thirty-two residents of La Paloma Flats were trapped on the wrong side of a washed-out bridge, and a sick child desperately need medical aid. Reaching the stub of the bridge, the ten members of the Search and Rescue unit split into two teams. One team would try to get a line across the bridge gap, while the other would go upstream and try to hop across the many debris piles in the rushing water.

The bridge team had early success by using a bow and arrow to shoot a fishing line across the gap. Successively larger lines were pulled across, until finally a taut cable was fixed, and a team member was able to hand-over-hand his way across the torrent. They would be able to retrieve the sick child.

The upstream team, which included Charles Rea, used equal ingenuity. Scrambling over loose and slippery debris piles they bridged the biggest stream torrent by cutting down a tree so that it fell across the gap, about four feet above the now rising water. They strung handlines across their makeshift bridge to create a walkway and Charles Rea got across. Rea clipped his safety harness onto the handline and started back across the slippery fallen tree. Halfway across he lost his footing and, still tethered to the handline, plunged into the water on the upstream side of the log and disappeared. Another team member scrambled out on the log where Rea's safety tether was attached and reached down into the raging water. At one point he felt Rea's hand, grabbed on and pulled with all his strength. The incredible power of the rushing water was holding Rea down, and no amount of pulling on Rea's arm or his safety harness could budge him. As team members frantically tried to pull Rea's body up, the rising water began to wash away the debris islands that were the team's bridge to safety, and even the log bridge began to shift. The anguished survivors had to retreat.

Agonized Montrose Search and Rescue members, along with Sheriffs and crews from the Forest Service spent hours trying to retrieve the body. Finally, the dam keeper upstream was able to temporarily cut off some of the flow from the dam, and the next day the water lowered enough to retrieve Rea's body.

Rea was a successful young man and left behind a wife and four young daughters. His loss, the first and only for the Montrose Search and Rescue Team, sobered our community, and reminded us what sacrifices they make for us.

The memorial itself was funded and built by local volunteers and contains stones from the site in the canyon where Charles Rea died. I hope you'll take the time to visit memorial and take time to honor the many men and women alive today who daily risk their lives for our safety.

---

1. Goldsworthy, Steve, interview by author.
2. Ibid.
3. Ibid.

Ice and Snow Rescues

CAMPERS SAVED BY THE WHISTLE

On Wednesday, January 2, 1974, John Larson took his three-year-old son John Junior on an adventure—a cold camping excursion into the San Gabriel Mountains. Larson was an experienced outdoorsman with proper gear. He planned to camp on a trail a few miles out of Buckhorn Campground, an area he was familiar with. He would return home Thursday or Friday.

On Wednesday morning Larson and his son pulled into the parking area just off Angeles Crest above Buckhorn. The sky was gray and light snow was a possibility, but it didn't look likely to Larson. The two hiked several miles down Buckhart Trail towards a waterfall in Cooper Canyon. As darkness approached they set up a tent trailside and crawled into their sleeping bags.

That night a snowstorm hit with unexpected intensity. When Larson and his young son woke up on Thursday, three feet of snow covered the trail. The snow was too deep for the boy to walk in, so Larson picked him up and began carrying him. With each step his legs sank into the deep snow, causing him to fall repeatedly. After 500 yards he knew he couldn't make it, and he decided to shelter in his tent and wait for help.

Back at home, Larson's wife Pam heard about the snowstorm and grew increasingly worried as Larson failed to show up. Friday morning, she called the Montrose Sheriffs. They dispatched Deputies up the Crest but they were unable to reach the campground. Rangers searched Buckhorn but found no campers and no car (the car was hidden under deep snow). As darkness fell, the call was put out for the Montrose Search and Rescue Team.

Inside the tent, now completely covered by the deep snow, Larson and his son were doing OK - warm sleeping bags, food and water. They sang songs, prayed, slept and waited.

On Saturday morning thirteen members of the Montrose Search and Rescue Team reached Buckhorn Campground. By early afternoon they found Larson's car when one of the sharp-eyed team members spotted the tip of the radio antenna poking out of a snowdrift. Deteriorating weather conditions and darkness forced the team back. The Larsons had been out four days now. The team knew their chances were getting slim.

Back in the tent, things were indeed getting critical. The warmth of the buried tent had melted snow beneath it, and an inch of icy water sloshed around the tent's floor. The sleeping bags were soaked and useless. Larson sat shivering on an upturned saucepan all Saturday night, cradling his exhausted boy in his arms. Frostbite was beginning to be inevitable.

Sunday morning the Montrose Search and Rescue and other searchers split into five teams and headed down different trails, shouting Larson's name. By afternoon, Larson realized they would die inside that tent. He had to dig himself out, even if he risked exposure. He slit the side of the tent and began tunneling out. As he dug he heard faint shouts. He pulled out a police whistle he had brought as part of his survival gear, and as he frantically dug, he blew the whistle with all his might. The Search and Rescue team could hear the barely audible sound of a whistle coming from what appeared to be just another big snow drift. They dug into the snow at the point they heard the sound and quickly reached the tunnel Larson was digging. They pulled Larson and son out of the hole, extremely wet and cold. The young boy, who had remained stoic and brave throughout the ordeal, burst into tears from the pent-up anxiety. While Larson was fitted with spare snowshoes, the boy was stuffed into one of the SAR team's backpacks. As it got dark, the group rendezvoused with a Highway Department Snow Weasel (an Army-surplus snow vehicle with tank-tracks). The Snow Weasel brought them back to Angeles Crest Highway, and four-wheel-drive vehicles took Larson and John Jr. to Verdugo Hills Hospital. Father and son were checked and released, and the Montrose SAR secured from another successful rescue. Larson and his son had been saved by their whistle.

Larson's son demonstrates blowing the whistle that saved their lives.

LITTLE GIRL'S PARENTS DISAPPEAR DOWN AN ICE-CHUTE

Our San Gabriel Mountains are treacherous enough with their steep mountainsides of slippery broken granite, but in the winter, a whole new range of dangers introduce themselves. A very deadly one is the phenomenon of "ice-chutes."

After each of our occasional snowstorms, a cycle of freeze-thaw, freeze-thaw occurs. The bright Southern California sun melts the snow each day, and after dark, the high-altitude freeze sets in, refreezing the melted snow. This cycle creates sheets of ice that are as slick as greased glass, and often times the ice sheets form on near-vertical slopes. Where the Angeles Crest Highway cuts across the slopes, these vertical ice sheets reach up onto the turnouts, creating slippery traps for the unwary who venture too close to the edge.

It happens again and again. A motorist pulls into a snowy turnout. They get out and walk to the edge to get a better view. They unknowingly step onto the glassy ice at the edge, and over they go. As they hurtle downward, they funnel into the gullies, the ice-chutes that create near-vertical toboggan runs. They pick up speed, flying down hundreds, sometimes thousands of feet at forty or fifty miles per hour, until they hit a tree or rock, usually ending in death.

Such were the conditions just before Christmas in 1982, when a mother, father, and their seven-year-old daughter drove up from the San Fernando Valley one afternoon to visit the snow. They pulled over into a snowy turnout at Dawson Saddle and got out to play in the snow. The father walked to the edge of the turnout where a steep cliff dropped off to a canyon far below. As the little girl watched, her father bent over to pick something up off the ground. To her horror, she saw his feet slip out from under him, and in a flash, he was gone over the side. The girl screamed to her mother that Dad had fallen and disappeared. Mom came running to the edge where Dad had been a moment before and leaned over the precipice to look for him. The same scene repeated itself for the panic-stricken girl. Mom's feet shot out from under her, and she too disappeared over the side and down the ice-chute.

A passing car noticed the car parked in the turnout, and saw the little girl in the back seat, with no one around. They pulled over, and the driver approached the car. The little girl appeared terrified and locked her doors. Not wanting to scare the girl the driver got back in his car and proceeded to the next turnout a short way up, where they pulled in. The two occupants got out and looked back. They could hear the girl screaming for her mother. When they happened to look down the cliff, they could see the form of the mother a few hundred feet below, so they called the Montrose Search and Rescue.

The MSR team had just finished retrieving two ice-chute fatalities the day before, two separate incidents that had happened in the same area. But they responded, and from the turnout, the team rappelled 300 feet down the slippery ice-chute in the dark. They found the woman alive but with massive head injuries. She had hit a rock and slammed up against a tree, stopping her from sliding further. She was strapped into a litter and winched up, to be airlifted out.

But the husband was nowhere to be seen. The MSR team searched the canyon below the ice-chute all that night in 20-degree weather. They were joined by rescue teams from Antelope Valley, San Dimas, Altadena, Sierra Madre, even far-away Malibu, until a total of thirty-nine men scoured the snow-bound canyon. Midday they finally found the father's broken and lifeless body in the snow a full quarter-mile from where he had started his horrible slide down the ice-chute.

These treacherous ice-chutes are a very real danger when it snows on the Angeles Crest Highway. Be wary of the edges of the highway in icy conditions.

In snow rescue training exercises, the team hones their rescue techniques with hundreds of hours of practice.

ICE RESCUES

In the last story, we learned about the treacherous ice-chutes that sometimes trap unwary visitors to our snowy mountains each winter. These slick, nearly vertical toboggan runs form in the turnouts along Angeles Crest Highway. Motorists sometimes stray too near to the edges and slide into the ice-chutes, often with fatal results. In 1981, two brothers stopped at an icy turnout of the Angeles Crest Highway to throw rocks off the edge. One brother slipped into an ice-chute and slid about 150 feet. The other brother tried to reach him but slid right past him to drop 1000 feet to his death. Another hiker faced a similar fate when he slipped off an icy cliff at Mt. Wilson. He too slid over 1000 feet but didn't die. MSR teams couldn't reach him from below, nor could a rescue chopper reach him, so he lay in the snow for six hours while an MSR team performed a grueling rope rappel down the icy cliff-face in the cold and dark to reach him.

The frequency of these ice cliff rescues prompted the team to acquire specialized training in ice climbing. MSR team member Mike Leum says:

> About ten years ago we were getting requested on Winter Ops to respond to Mt. Baldy on a regular basis. Frequently, these were for recoveries of hikers who had fallen down ice-chutes, sometimes at a distance of 1,000 feet. I realized that we could only safely check the tops and bottoms of these chutes. Also, during one of those searches I fell at the summit of Mt. Baldy and had to use my ice axe to stop my fall. I was on my back going headfirst downslope. That combination of events led me to get some vertical ice training from the American Alpine Institute.[1]

The training with the American Alpine Institute has turned into a yearly pilgrimage for the MSR team. Each winter they drive to the eastern Sierras, and climb through deep snow into the higher elevations, to the 10,000-foot level. In Lee Vining Canyon north of Mammoth, with guides from the Alpine Institute, they challenge a 200-foot frozen waterfall, climbing the slick vertical face in near zero-degree weather. Under the tutelage of their guides they learn to set ice screws into the vertical face and attach ropes to the screws until each climber is secured at four points and tied to the other climbers. With cramp-ons on their boots and specialized ice axes they make their way up the face to the next attach point. It is an extremely technical climbing technique.

MSR Team member Steve Goldsworthy says, "If you can safely climb ninety degrees, then doing an ice rescue on a 60-degree slope seems a lot easier. I guess the real danger is the unforgiving nature of ice. One slip, one fall, has often fatal results."

The training does carry dangers. During one exercise, Mike Leum was climbing the face of the waterfall, when the ice sheet he was on shattered. The climber below him was showered with broken ice and a large piece clipped his hand, breaking the bones. Mike had fallen, dropped past the climber below, and dangled by the ropes of his other attach points, sixty feet above the ground. Despite immense pain, the man with the broken hand was able to lower Mike safely to the ground. The team is built on training and trust.

The MSR is one of the few search and rescue teams to have this kind of specialized training and they are well-known as the "Vertical Ice Response Team." One example of the team's training having paid off happened at Mt. Baden-Powell. A young man and his girlfriend tried to climb a vertical ice sheet from Angeles Crest Highway. At the 400-foot level, the man slipped and slid all the way to the highway where he died on impact. The girl was left terrified and clinging to a tree growing out of the cliff face. The Vertical Ice Response Team was able to quickly climb straight up the ice sheet and lower the girl to safety. The MSR's ice climbing training saved a life that day.

Opposite page: Using specialized ice-climbing equipment a MSR team member climbs the slick vertical face of a frozen waterfall. This is the ultimate in specialized climbing and comes in handy for winter rescues in the steep San Gabriel Mountains.

After a successful 200-foot climb, a team member rappels back down. This once-a-year training makes the Montrose Search and Rescue team one of the only vertical ice rescue teams in the nation.

The team climbs the frozen waterfall, one man above the other, tethered to the top by safety ropes.

RESCUE OF SNOWBOUND SCOUT TROOP YIELDS GRISLY DISCOVERY

In January of 1988, two different Boy Scout troops were getting experience in cold-weather camping in the San Gabriel Mountains when an unexpectedly powerful storm blew in, dropping a heavy covering of snow. Troop 108 from Culver City had parked their cars on a turnout of Angeles Crest Highway, and then hiked about a mile down to Buckhorn Campground to camp the night. When they awoke in the morning to the raging storm, the three adult Scout leaders and eleven Scouts, aged eleven to fifteen, broke camp and slowly made their way back to their cars. The winds were gusting at 40 mph and snowdrifts were as high as four feet. When they did reach the cars, there was no way the cars would be able to move, so they sheltered inside them for several hours. A group of recreational 4WD vehicles came upon them and gave them a lift to safety.

Higher up the Crest another Scout troop from Palos Verdes had spent the night at Little Jimmy Campground. After a sleepless night in their tents listening to the raging storm, the four adult leaders and twenty-one Scouts broke camp and waded three miles through deep snow to their pre-arranged pick-up point at Islip Saddle. The bus to pick them up had gotten no further than Chilao, and from there the driver had telephoned for assistance from the Montrose Search and Rescue.

MSR responded, setting up at Newcomb's Ranch with vans to take the Scouts out once they were found. Two patrol teams were sent in vehicles up the unplowed snow-bound highway. One team paused just past the tunnels on the way to Islip Saddle, while the other team went further up on foot. The two members of the team by the tunnel noticed an odd lump in the snow, and when they got closer, they could see it was a car, completely covered in a snow-drift.

The two MSR members dug the snow away from the doors, and peering through the car's windows could see three people inside, appearing to be asleep. Not able to get a response from the car's occupants, the rescuers broke the windows of the car, and reached inside. The three people inside were cold and stiff.

Just at this point, the Scout troop found by rescuers a few hundred yards up the road at Islip, came trudging up to the scene. The MSR members hurriedly covered the car so the kids wouldn't witness the grisly discovery. After the Scouts had been escorted by the car and ferried down to Newcomb's for the trip home, the team dove into recovering the bodies from the car. The three bodies were two young men, eighteen and twenty-four years old and a seventeen-year-old girl. They appeared peaceful, just sleeping, which is a common appearance with carbon monoxide poisoning. The car's ignition was on, and the heater was all the way on, but the gas tank was empty, indicating they had been there for many hours, perhaps even since the day before. It also appeared that the car's front wheels were stuck in the ditch at the side of the road. It was surmised that a simple drive to the snow had turned deadly when, perhaps in turning around, the car became stuck. The group had apparently decided to sleep in the idling car overnight with the heater on. When snow covered the car's exhaust during the night, the heater blower probably funneled the exhaust into the car's interior, and the group died in their sleep.

It was noted that at the time of the discovery, the car was almost completely covered by snow, and it was still snowing. Even after snowplowing the road, the car in the ditch may not have been found for several days. The coroner wasn't able make it to the snowbound location to handle the bodies, so the MSR team reluctantly extracted the bodies and loaded them into the back of their rescue truck for the long ride down the hill to Verdugo Hills Hospital. A successful Scout rescue had brought about a sad discovery.

TRAPPED IN A SNOW AVALANCHE ON ANGELES CREST

We have such a friendly familiarity with the mountains above us that we forget that nature up there can be deadly. In April of 1967, Mother Nature played an April Fool's Day joke on the southland by bringing a frigid storm to LA on April 1 that included rain, hail, sleet, wind, and a huge amount of snow to the San Gabriel Mountains.

A few days after the storm La Crescenta resident Alvin Lewison and his wife Ruth decided to take advantage of the newly snow-plowed Angeles Crest Highway for a drive through a rare local winter scene. They were headed to Rialto to visit friends and planned to transit the Crest Highway past Wrightwood and come back down Route 66 in the Cajon Pass. The highway must have been spectacular, with deep drifts on either side, and others were taking in the beauty as well.

At 3 p.m. they were in a clumped line of cars winding slowly through the white wonderland, about eight miles from Big Pines. Without warning the cars were buffeted by tons of snow, roaring down the mountainside and over the road. A snowy avalanche had broken loose from the mountainside and covered the group of cars. They were all trapped. There was no way to know when someone would come upon them or report them overdue. Darkness was approaching quickly, and I'm sure many in the caravan weren't prepared for an overnight in sub-zero temperatures.

But fortunately for the group, Alvin Lewison was a HAM radio operator, and kept a mobile unit in his car. As we know today, cell phones would have been useless in condition like this, but HAM radios have a unique ability to work in conditions that render normal communication systems, like telephones, useless. HAM radios are still called on today to transmit important information during and after disasters, such as Hurricane Katrina or the 9-11 terrorist attacks. Alvin Lewison at the time of the avalanche was tuned to the West Coast Amateur Radio Service Net (WECARS) which is monitored by amateur radio operators to provide service to motorists, by contacting the Highway Patrol or the Auto Club. From his buried car Alvin was able to connect with HAM operators in Hollywood, South Pasadena, King City in Central California, and Daly City near San Francisco. The County Sheriff was called, and MSR rescuers driving behind a snow plow were dispatched from the La Canada end of the highway.

Darkness fell, but soon the headlights of the approaching rescue team were spotted. Three of the cars were able to be extricated from the snow, and the tired and cold group started the long journey back down to LA. They had crawled barely three miles down the road when a second avalanche crossed the highway in front of them, blocking the road. The caravan now turned around and headed back towards the spot where they had been trapped earlier. They dug past that and continued in the darkness toward Wrightwood. Near Big Pines, the lead car's headlights suddenly illuminated a steel barrier that had been erected across the highway. Everyone hit their brakes hard, as the lead car and the following vehicles skidded wildly into the snowbanks on either side. Everyone made it through this last scare, and the cars continued down the mountain, through the Cajon Pass, and back to LA. The Lewisons got home to La Crescenta at 3 a.m.

Another sidelight of the HAM radio adventure: One of the Deputy Sheriffs in the rescue party had a very pregnant wife at home, who had no way of knowing where her husband was when he didn't return for dinner that night. Alvin was able to reach a HAM operator in Palos Verdes, who telephoned the officer's wife to let her know where her husband was and approximately when he'd be home. This group of avalanche victims was fortunate one in their group was prepared for an emergency. For CV's Lewison family, Alvin's HAM hobby had saved the day.

OUT-OF-BOUNDS SKIERS PAY FOR THEIR RESCUE

It was the last run of a snowy day of skiing back in February of 1998, when two snowboarders crossed the marked boundaries of the ski run into fresh snow. They said it was accidental, that they didn't see the signs that warned skiers not to cross over. But cross over they did, and they spent the next twenty-four hours fighting for their lives.

According to the pair, they became disoriented in fog, and couldn't find their way back to the Snow Crest ski resort in the Mt. Waterman area. They found shelter in a small cave or overhang, found dry wood, and started a fire with a lighter and money from their wallets. Wandering on the next day, they abandoned their snowboards, and one of them took a tumble off a seventy-foot cliff, dislocating his hip.

It just so happened that the Montrose Search and Rescue Team was in the mountains for snow and ice training that day, so when the call came for the missing snowboarders, they were close at hand. The case took on particular urgency as another snowboarder had gotten lost just a couple weeks earlier. In that tragic case the snowboarder died.

About sixty-five searchers, made up of MSR, ski patrol and law officers combed the area around the ski runs. MSR team members strapped on snowshoes and started walking through the knee-deep snow, trying to follow the tracks of the lost snowboarders. As light dawned the next day, a helicopter spotted the discarded snowboards, and by afternoon the two lost skiers had been located about four miles from the resort.

The two were initially grateful and appreciative. Immediately after their rescue, the papers quote the two as saying: "I won't be doing much out-of-bounds snowboarding. You see your life flash in front of you. It's a dumb thing to do." And "If I have to reimburse them, it will be well worth it. They saved our lives and saved our families a lot of grief."

That all changed when criminal charges were leveled at the pair. The snowboarders were charged with trespassing. Although the MSR has a policy of not charging for their rescues, the County District Attorney felt otherwise, and was asking for restitution of $23,000 to cover the basic costs of the rescue operation. However, the county would not seek jail time.

Despite their earlier statement of willingness to pay for their rescue, the pair decided to dispute the fine. The case went to trial in July, and the two snowboarders fought the misdemeanor trespassing charges on the grounds that the out-of-bounds area had not been properly marked by the ski resort. A couple of the MSR search team members had to testify in the trial, based on their report that the two had verbally admitted to skiing out-of-bounds when they were rescued, which the two contested. The defense lawyer claimed that his clients had been bullied into a confession.

Although these technicalities were argued, for the jury it was a simple matter. They had to merely decide if the two had gone out-of-bounds intentionally. A juror on the case later said:

> We felt that they did go out of bounds to look for fresh powder to ski on. There were signs posted and the trails were so that you couldn't go out of bounds without knowing it. It's just like if there's a 'no parking' sign. You don't park!

Despite their protestations, the two were found guilty of trespassing and fined $23,000 for restitution. Ironically, one of the two guilty snowboarders was not present when the verdict was read, as he was at an LAPD training event as part of his quest to become a police officer.

Above: The team huddles over maps as they communicate with searchers on the mountain looking for the lost snowboarders.

Below: A rescuer from the team trudges through deep snow.

One of the lost snowboarders, accompanied by his family, enters the Crescenta Valley Sheriff Station after his rescue.

Again, the MSR does not, by policy, charge for their rescues. But this rescue had involved sixty-five volunteers, police and firemen, along with a helicopter for a 24-hour period of bad weather, with risk of avalanche. The LA County Sheriff Department spokesman said of the decision to seek restitution: "This was an intentional criminal act, and the taxpayers should not have to pay."

---

1. Leum, Mike, interview by author.

Car Crash Rescues

FOUR DAYS IN A CRASHED CAR

Often the tales of survival by accident victims are as fascinating as the stories of their rescues. In 1984 a young woman miraculously survived for nearly four days after running her car off the edge of the highway and down into a ravine. She was within earshot of the Angeles Crest Highway and was only discovered by accident.

On the evening of October 25, 1984, Lori had a nasty fight with her husband at their home in Eagle Rock. Lori, who was barefoot at the time, angrily left the house and jumped in her mini pickup for a drive up the dark Angeles Crest Highway. She had only gone a couple of miles, just past the ranger station, when her truck went over the side. Lori stated later that she lost control of the truck because of bald tires, but the CHP investigation showed she was probably in the process of turning around and accidentally backed off the side of the turnoff. The truck tumbled and slid about 150 feet down the steep mountainside before finally coming to rest upside down, wedged in heavy brush. Lori had hurt her back and banged her head but was conscious. It was pitch dark and cold, about forty degrees, and as far as Lori knew, no one knew where she had gone, and no one saw her go off the edge.

Lori's mind went into survival mode. She was injured, she was barefoot, and would never get out of there without shoes. Like many people's cars, she had a lot of junk in her vehicle. In the dark, she found a roll of electrical tape. She tore off sections of her seat cover and fashioned a pair of makeshift shoes.

When reading these rescue stories, one must keep in mind the extreme nature of the terrain in our mountains. The slope her truck rested on was nearly vertical and made up of decomposed granite and rocks that would slide downward at the slightest touch. Below the truck was nearly impenetrable brush, growing out of the same slippery material. She tried for several hours to climb back up to the roadway, but every agonizing step up just sent her sliding downward. She went back to her truck and gathered some blankets, along with a pencil and paper to keep a diary in case she didn't get out alive. Next, she tried sliding downslope from her truck. Weakened and injured, she quickly became mired in the dense brush, no longer able to move either up or down. She lay trapped in the brush for 3 and a half days, in agony and fully expecting to die. She kept notes in her homemade diary for her family to read after her body was found.

Cars that fly off the edge of the treacherous Angeles Crest Highway are difficult to deal with. After rappelling down the slope to a wrecked vehicle, this MSR team member yells up to his team above.

Power tools have been brought down to this wreck site, and team members are cutting their way into the car.

A crash victim is carefully extricated from wreckage.

A victim in a litter is winched up with an assist from a MSR team member, just as Lori would have been.

Lori's pickup truck is winched back up to the highway after her rescue.

A few days later, the big Sheriff rescue chopper was on its way to its base camp at Barley Flats, when one of the crewmen spotted an overturned vehicle in the brush below the highway. They set down at a turnout for a routine check. The crest was a favorite dumping ground for stolen cars, and that's what they expected to find, a stripped hulk. But when they reached the truck after rappelling down the slope, they could make out a weak voice below them calling for help.

Montrose Search and Rescue Team rappelled down another 500 feet down through dense brush to Lori, where they found her very weak, but still alert. The team strapped her to a stretcher and winched her to the top of a nearby ridge. The same helicopter that spotted her truck came in carefully for a tricky one-wheel landing. The big chopper planted one landing gear on the ridgetop, and the team slid her stretcher quickly into the open door.

Lori was treated at Verdugo Hills Hospital, where doctors reported that she was elated to have survived. Her diary recorded her extreme hunger and thirst, along with her pain from injuries. She was convinced that she wouldn't be rescued, and that she would die of thirst. The rescue team deemed it a miracle she was found, noting that had the truck slid another fifteen feet, it would have been completely engulfed in brush and invisible from above. It was indeed a miracle that she was found, and a miracle that she survived at all.

SAVED FROM DEATH, ETERNALLY GRATEFUL

One March evening in 2012, a late snowstorm had blanketed the San Gabriel Mountains. Tracy Granger, fifty-six, was driving from Pasadena to her home in Palmdale, taking the Angeles Crest Highway. As she rounded a curve in the darkness, she hit a patch of ice, and broke loose. Her pickup truck spun toward the road's edge, and she knew she was going over the side. The truck plummeted violently 350 feet down the sheer mountainside finally stopping, deeply imbedded in brush. She had whacked her head hard, broken her neck, pelvis and several ribs. Her body had been slammed about, but she was still conscious, sitting in the driver's seat, looking up the cliff toward the highway, where through the heavy brush she could see the lights of passing cars.

She knew she had to get up to the highway or she'd never be found. Opening the truck's door, she painfully pried herself out, only to make an agonizing fall into the snow, where she lay immobile. She was now in the snow, in freezing cold, critically injured, in just a light sweatshirt. Tracy reported later that as she faded into unconsciousness, she reached out to her husband telepathically, saying out loud, "Lee, I'm overdue. Something has happened. Figure it out." Apparently, it worked, and her husband called the Sheriff.

The Montrose Search and Rescue Team was called out, knowing only that Tracy had disappeared somewhere between Pasadena and Palmdale. They were also faced with the dilemma of looking for a white vehicle in the white snow. They began to drive the Crest looking for any sign of her. As daybreak broke, a helicopter joined the search. At 9:30 a.m. one of the MSR members spotted something from the rescue truck, perhaps the faint traces of tire tracks headed off the edge of the road. He scanned the terrain below and was barely able to see the white vehicle buried in the snow-covered bushes.

Knowing Tracy had been there all night, he grabbed his medical bag, and with no ropes, plunged over the side. After a controlled slide down the sheer face he reached Tracy, lying in the snow. She had succumbed to hypothermia, but the rescuer could detect a very faint pulse. He called up to his partners that she was still alive. They grabbed more medical gear, and jumped over the side, also without ropes. The three MSR rescuers began first aid. Within ten minutes,

The big rescue helicopter slides carefully into a narrow canyon.

Only five months after the accident that nearly took her life, Tracy Granger (in pink) rappels down to her crash site, accompanied by her rescuers.

the big rescue helicopter had slid into the narrow canyon, and Tracy was winched up. Tracy Granger was deep in severe hypothermia, her body temperature at eighty-five degrees. She flat-lined three times in the helicopter but came back, due largely to the first aid given by the rescue team. Amazingly she recovered.

These are the kinds of rescues the MSR team lives for. For Tracy had not only survived her brush with death, but she was determined to show her gratitude to her life-saving rescuers in an unusual way. When the rescue team visited Tracy in the hospital a month later, she vowed to return with them to the scene of the accident to bring attention to the heroic rescue they had performed. Sure enough, in August of 2012, only five months after her accident, the still healing woman accompanied the MSR team up the Crest to the accident site, followed by news vans. As news cameras recorded the event, Tracy Granger rappelled down the hillside, along with the team that had saved her life, to visit the exact spot she had almost died. There she found two things: a shirt she had been wearing that night, and the chilling realization that had her truck not stopped where it did, there were hundreds more feet to fall. There were tears and hugs as she posed for photos with her rescuers. She was intensely grateful to the team.

In November 2012, those same eleven members of MSR team were awarded the Sheriff Department Lifesaving Award and honored with the Rescue of the Year. And Tracy Granger was there to hand out the awards to the heroes that had saved her life.

CAR OVER! DID THAT REALLY HAPPEN?

The Angeles Crest Highway has beckoned to car drivers and motorcycle riders since it was opened decades ago. Its twisting hairpin turns coupled with thousand feet drop-offs just inches beyond the thin guardrail have created a recipe for disaster for anyone too drunk or too heavy on the throttle. Literally thousands of cars and bikes have sailed off the edge. The Montrose Search and Rescue Team have been the ones that have had to go find them and haul them back up to the road. Many of the crashes are tragic, but a few are almost absurd.

On a January evening in 1984, a young man and a friend bought some dinner and took it to one of the many turnouts on Angeles Crest to eat while watching the twinkling city lights. The stillness was broken by the sound of a high-powered car roaring up the highway toward the turnout. The engine revved higher as it approached the turnout. Suddenly its headlights veered wildly, and the speeding car spun out, leaving the highway and entering the turnout. The car flashed past the young man's car, barely missing it, and skidded past two other parked cars, before sailing off the edge and disappearing. It happened so fast that the young man could hardly believe what had just happened.

As silence again descended on the dark turnout, the man jumped out of his car and ran to the spot that the car had gone over. There was no sound and no trace of the car. It was almost as if he had just imagined it. After shouting down the cliff with no response, he drove back down the highway, and banged on the door of the first house he came to (pre-cellphone days) to call for help.

MSR responded, and after a very difficult rappel nearly 500 feet down the sheer cliff-face through dense brush, they found the driver of the crashed car. He was injured but alive, and his car was another 100 feet down. The MSR winched the driver back up to the turnout, as proof to the accident witness that he had actually seen the split-second crash.

The tangled wreckage of a car is brought up as a California Highway Patrol officer looks on. This kind of massive damage is typical of cars that go tumbling down hundreds of feet after going over the side of Angeles Crest Highway.

Skid marks and a broken guard rail are sometimes the only indicators of a crash site, when cars go off the edge unseen.

An incredibly mangled car is winched back up to the highway. It's easy to see why many times crashes like this are fatal.

Need a lift? This is the type of winching equipment used by the Montrose Search and Rescue team to bring crash victims up hundreds of feet.

JPL COMMUTER VAN GOES OFF THE CREST

Many people take commuter vans to ease their commute. They are often driven by the commuters themselves, sometimes on a rotating basis. On a cold morning in December of 2004, ten employees of JPL boarded their white commuter van in Lancaster for the long ride to JPL in La Canada. Sometimes they took the crowded 14 Freeway, but more often they took the winding Angeles Forest Highway, a quicker route.

It was a tight group of regulars who had become close over their many months of daily commuting. Most of them were churchgoers and discussed church activities on their ride. Some slept. All were friends. "We had a ball in the van," one of them said later. "A lot of joking would go on, kidding around with each other." But the group was quieter than normal on this trip, and maybe that was part of the problem. Most of them were asleep when halfway through the trip, the driver closed his eyes for just a second and drifted off. The road curved left, but the van went straight.

The van hit the berm at the side of the road hard, waking everyone up in time to see the edge of the highway disappear behind them, and in a flash, everything was spinning. The van was rolling over and over 400 feet down the hillside, glass flying, people screaming and crying. When the van finally stopped rolling it was upright, but the roof had crushed down to the level of the seats. Some of the passengers were wedged down tight against their seats, unable to move. The driver was trapped beneath the crushed roof. His neck was broken but he was still conscious, although insensible. He honked the horn repeatedly. One woman was laid out on a bench seat, unable to move, her back broken. Blood began to pool on the floor of the van. Only one of the ten was able to extricate himself, and although injured, he painfully tried to climb back the slippery hillside for help.

Fortunately for those still alive in the van, help was not far away. A car happened to be right behind the van when it went off the side. The driver stopped, but having no cell service and seeing there was nothing he could do, he sped ahead and amazingly, found a CHP unit just one mile away. The call was put out and help streamed in from all quarters. First on the scene was a Forest Service employee, who began scrambling down the slope. He could hear the van's horn honking, and he met the one victim trying to climb up, who called to him to help his friends. When he arrived at the van he could hear shouts for help coming from inside the crushed vehicle, but there was no way to get to them.

Soon the Highway Patrol, the Montrose Search and Rescue Team, and other rescue services arrived. Power cutters were carried down to the van and the survivors began to slowly get cut out of the wreckage. Three helicopters hovered overhead, and as each victim was cut out they were strapped in a litter and winched up to a waiting chopper. It took several hours to get the seven survivors out and to the hospital, and even more time to pull the three dead out. All of the victims that were found alive eventually recovered.

It had been a miracle that someone saw the accident and, in an area with no cell reception, that the authorities were alerted so quickly. Many more would have died had more time passed. In this case, with so many gruesome injuries, a call was put out for a Sheriff Department psychologist to come to the scene and talk with the team members after they had secured from the rescue. The MSR pays a great price psychologically when they deal with accidents like this one.

In this grainy view from a news helicopter, we see how the commuter van's roof has been flattened to the bottom of the van's window frames.

Thrilling Tales of the Montrose Search and Rescue

A rescue helicopter winches up another injured victim up from the crash site.

After bringing them up the slope from the crash site, the Montrose Search and Rescue team carries one of the crash victims to a helicopter. The stress from witnessing such massive carnage is evident on their faces.

Dog Rescues

THE MONTROSE SEARCH AND RESCUE, A DOG'S BEST FRIEND

While the MSR team's efforts are focused on human rescues, they do honor the fact that many dog owners consider their pets as one of the family. The MSR rescues about a half-dozen dogs each year. The following are a sampling of some of those rescues.

In the winter of 1992 the MSR team was on a routine snow rescue training exercise up at Krakta Ridge in the Angeles National Forest. Near to their exercise area, a golden retriever puppy playing in the new snow got too close to the edge of a ravine and slid 1,000 feet down an icy slope. The team linked together their rescue ropes and lowered a team member down to the puppy. The uninjured and grateful puppy was placed in a backpack and pulled back up.

In 1976, a hiker watched in horror as his small dog slipped off the edge of a steep trail in Big Tujunga Canyon. The dog stopped sliding about seventy-five feet down. After several abortive attempts to reach him, the hiker drove to a Ranger station, and he and the Ranger attempted another failed rescue. The MSR team was finally called, and with no trouble at all, reached the dog, placed him in a sling and brought him back up. At the top, the grateful dog walked up to each MSR team member and thanked them with a wag of his tail.

A not-so-grateful dog was rescued with his owner after a 250-foot tumble off the edge of the Angeles Crest Highway just above La Canada. Just before nightfall, the dog slipped on the edge and began sliding down. His owner grabbed for him, lost his balance and tumbled past his dog, stopping at about thirty-five feet. He looked up just in time to see his dog rolling down the slope towards him. As the dog went by, he grabbed him, but the big dog's momentum pulled them both rolling and tumbling another 200 feet. The dog was uninjured, but the owner's hip was dislocated, and he was unable to climb. As darkness fell and the cold came on, the protective dog snuggled to provide warmth to his injured owner. Finally, at 11:30 p.m. a passing motorist who had pulled off the road heard the man's calls for help.

The MSR winched a rescue team down the steep hill. It was at this point that the confused and traumatized dog decided to go into protective mode, and he wouldn't let the team get near his owner. After some painful jockeying around, the injured owner was finally able to get his faithful dog leashed and subdued. The injured man was strapped to a stretcher, and holding his dog, he was winched back up the steep slope.

The team uses their training to pull the linked ropes attached to the puppy and his rescuer 1,000 feet up the icy slope.

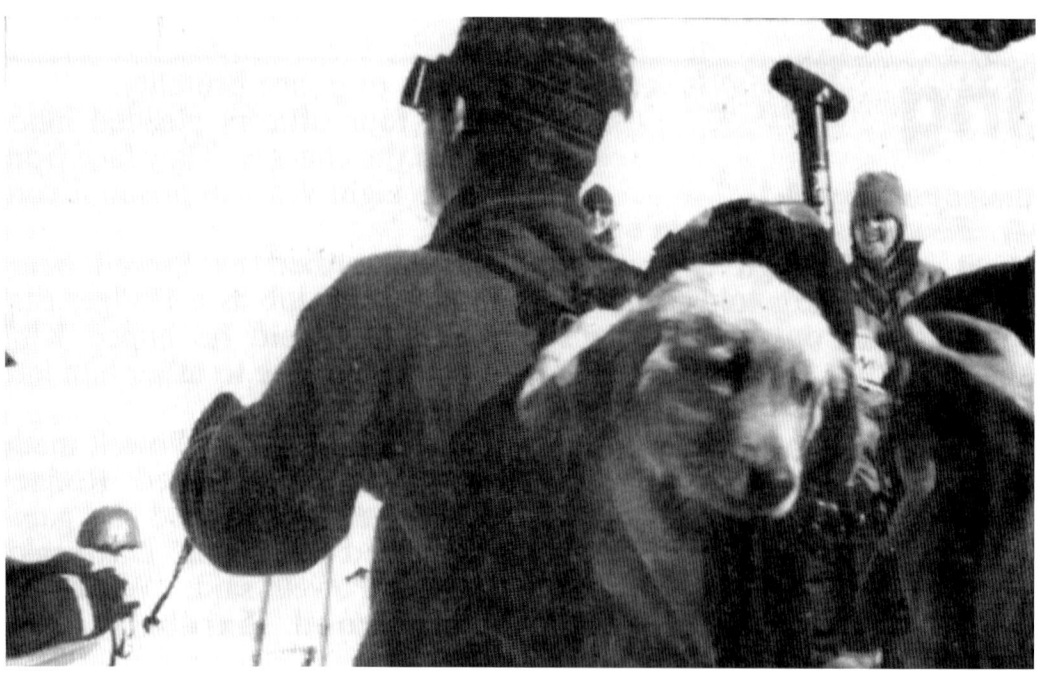

The puppy seems to be smiling as he reaches the top of the cliff, safely riding in his rescuer's backpack.

Dog Rescues

A grateful Golden Retriever licks the hands of the team that saved his life.

Another man, Chuck, took his two German shepherds down into the narrows area of Big Tujunga Canyon for a play-day by the river. The playful dogs got further down the canyon than Chuck was comfortable with., but when he called them back, the rambunctious dogs got caught in the river's strong current and swept downstream. They fetched up on a ledge of rock in the center of the stream just above a waterfall, where they were trapped. Chuck followed them down and tried to carry them off the rock. Chuck remembers: "I was constantly going under and trying to hold the dogs up. I saw their claws bleeding. It was deep in both directions. They couldn't go anywhere else."

After six hours of trying to retrieve his dogs himself, darkness began to fall, and Chuck went for help, leaving his dogs behind. "I cried all the way up", Chuck said later. Battered, wet and cold, he stumbled into the Hidden Springs Café, where the call went out to the MSR. After a three-hour hike by the rescue team, the dogs were pulled off the ledge and returned to Chuck. "I didn't know the Montrose Search and Rescue did things like that," said a grateful Chuck. We're glad, and grateful, that they do.

Continuing with some other dog rescues performed by the Montrose Search and Rescue Team, we look no further than Pickens Canyon in March of 1991. Two young boys, best friends, were hiking the canyon at dusk. As often happens to young boys, they stayed out too long, and darkness overtook them. Wrong turns in the dark with no flashlights took them down a steep incline, only to get trapped on a ledge with a 90-foot drop below them. With no way up and no way down, they were left with just one option: sit down in the dark and wait.

They were both scared but were confident their parents would find them. Sure enough, they soon heard their parents calling their names, and were able to establish voice contact with them.

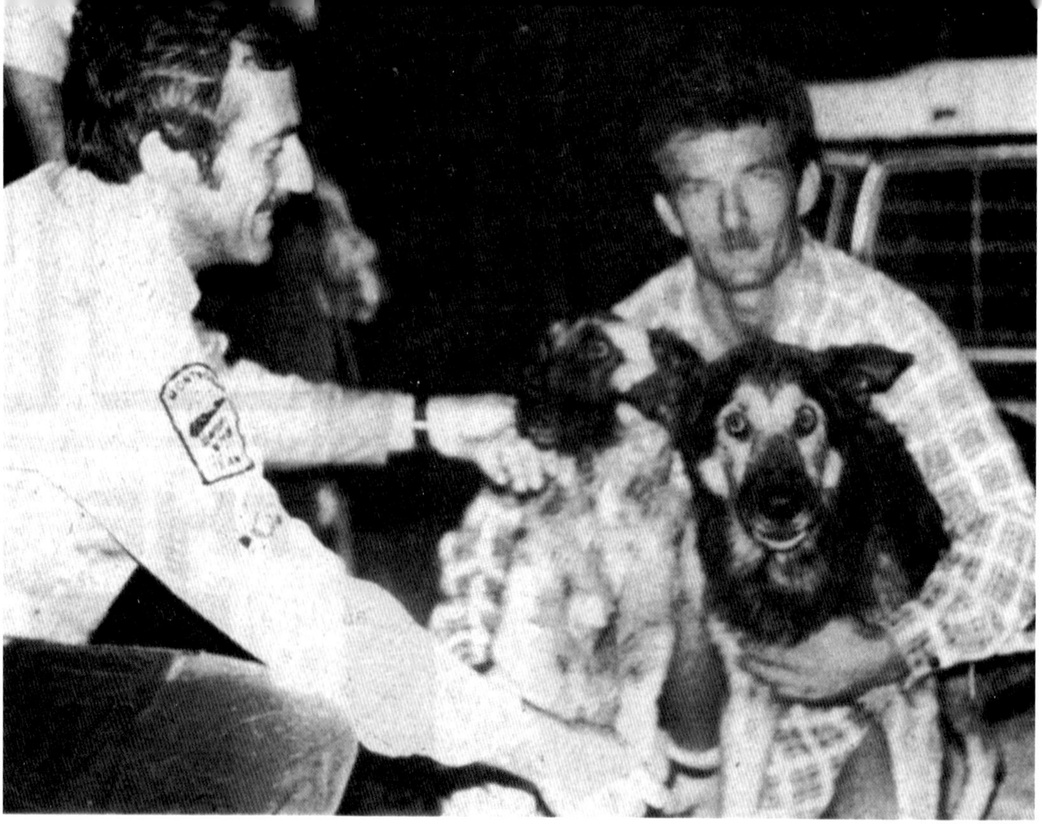

Above: A grateful Chuck holds his two exhausted German Shepherds after a grueling rescue. "I didn't know the Montrose Search and Rescue did things like that!"

Left: The two rescued boys crouch down with their faithful dog Tassha near the spot they were trapped.

One of the boys' pets, a Golden Retriever named Tassha was with the parents, and she wasn't going to let the boys sit out there alone. She scrambled down to the two boys and sat patiently with them while the parents went for help.

Soon the cliff face was illuminated by the spotlights of two helicopters, while the MSR came in by foot. They set up a rope system and lowered the boys and their dog down the cliff one-by-one. The dog was described as "real cooperative." News vans waited at the bottom of the canyon to interview the boys, but Tassha got all the attention. One of the boys joked, "I was bummed out 'cause they cut me off the broadcast. My dog got on TV, but I didn't!"

A sad but poignant story took place in Big Tujunga Canyon one Sunday in September of 1988. A young Tujunga man was walking with Clyde, his nine-year-old Doberman, near the highway by Narrows Bridge. The dog fell off the side of the road and went down a sheer cliff several hundred feet. The man called to his dog but could hear no response. There was no trail down, and it was very steep. Not knowing what to do, he drove back home for help. Accompanied now by his step-father he returned to try to get down to his dog. He panicked and tried to go down the sheer canyon face after him, but the cliff was just too steep. He too began sliding down but was able to grab onto a rock outcropping after sliding thirty feet. His stepfather on the road above was able to flag down a passing Forest Service vehicle, who called for the MSR.

As darkness fell the big rescue chopper came in and lowered two paramedics to the dog owner, clinging to his precarious handhold. He was treated for minor injuries, cuts and scrapes, and was winched back up to the chopper. The chopper's crew could see the dog on the canyon floor, crumpled and motionless, clearly dead, but because of darkness and low fuel they opted not to retrieve the body.

The next morning, Monday, the grieving dog owner returned to try to figure a way down to retrieve his pet's body. As he told a local newspaper, "They won't get my dog, so I got to go back and get him. He's my best friend!" The dog owner, more cautious now after his rescue the day before, gave up, but vowed, "I'm not an experienced climber, and yet I got to go back to him. I have to bury him. I just can't leave him there. It's just not right."

On late Tuesday, the MSR, fearing the man would injure himself trying to retrieve his beloved pet's body, returned to the scene on foot. Rappelling down the cliff they found the dog's body and raised it back up to the road for the grieving owner to bury.

For so many of us, our dogs and cats are family members. We're glad that the Montrose Search and Rescue members feel the same. Although their first priority is human life, they still find time and energy to help out our loyal pets.

RESCUING THE MAYOR'S DOG

In November of 2002, there was a particularly high-profile dog rescue. Former Glendale Mayor Sheldon Baker lives on the edge of Brand Park with his wife and two small house-dogs. One Saturday morning, an accidently open back door provided an escape path for the two dogs, who took off into the Verdugo Mountains above Brand Park for a little adventure. But only one dog came back that afternoon. The Bakers, along with friends, searched the hills in the direction the dogs had gone. Frustratingly they could hear the little dog barking off in the distance, but the sound bouncing off the canyon walls and the steep terrain kept them from homing in on the thirteen-month-old Sheltie. Darkness made them retreat from their search Saturday night. The Bakers agonized over the fate of their beloved pet, sure that coyotes would finish off the dog in the night.

They resumed the search Sunday morning, and amazingly could once again hear the poor little lost dog barking in the distance. Another day of fruitless and frustrating searching turned up nothing, as once again the terrain made pinpointing the dog's barking impossible. Yet another day and night passed.

On Monday evening, Baker hiked one last time into the hills, sure that his pet was dead by now. Incredibly, he could hear the dog barking weakly. In desperation Sheldon Baker called the cellphone of his old friend, Mike Leum of the Montrose Search and Rescue, not for help, but for advice on what to do next. Mike was at Tam O' Shanter Inn, a high-end restaurant, enjoying dinner with his wife for their thirteenth wedding anniversary. Mike took the call from his good friend Baker, who had been Mike's Scoutmaster when he was in Boy Scouts. Mike told Baker that given the amount of time the dog had been missing, he would call out the team immediately. He further assured Baker that the team often does animal rescues. He left his incredibly understanding wife, and joined eight other team members at Baker's house, where they embarked into the hills.

In a short time, the team, with their superior tracking skills and night-vision goggles spotted the dog trapped on a small ledge halfway down a sheer cliff. There was no way that anyone would be able to climb up the unstable hillside, so the team opted to rappel down from the top. After breaking through thick brush, they finally reached the weakened dog, and carried him back up to safety.

According to Mike Leum, the dog had probably fallen off the top of the ridge and tumbled until it landed on the tiny outcropping. Ironically it was the inaccessibility of the spot the dog was stuck in that saved its life. The dog's barking must have sounded like a dinner-bell to every coyote and bobcat for miles around, but they couldn't cross the sheer cliff-face to get to the trapped animal.

The tiny dog, one and a half pounds lighter from its ordeal, and hopefully a little wiser, resumed its quiet life as a house-dog in the home of the former Mayor. And Sheldon Baker and family will always be indebted to our local heroes.

Dog Rescues

Right: A team member carries the mayor's exhausted dog after two and a half days trapped on a ledge.

Below: A grateful Mayor Baker poses with the team after his dog's recue.

Plane Crash Rescues

PLANE DOWN IN DUNSMORE CANYON

On a very foggy morning in June of 1969, three thirteen-year-old boys set out on a hike up Dunsmore Canyon, known today as Deukmejian Wilderness Park. At the same time at Van Nuys Airport, four young college students, one of them an inexperienced pilot, climbed into a single engine plane for a sight-seeing flight to the Grand Canyon. They didn't comprehend that a thick fog bank barred their way over the San Gabriel Mountains.

The three young hikers had just begun their ascent of the rocky canyon. The fog was extremely thick. They could see only a few feet ahead. At 8:55 a.m. they heard the sound of an airplane getting louder and louder as it approached. The plane roared right over their heads, maybe 100 feet above, and for just a second, they could see the misty outline of the plane. The engine sound continued up the canyon ahead of them, then suddenly went silent, followed immediately by a bang, like a car door being slammed.

The boys ran back down the canyon to Markridge Avenue and found a Fire Department call box. Both County and Glendale Fire units responded and began to pick their way up the rough fire roads on the canyon floor and on the rocky, chaparral-covered ridges above. They had no idea where the plane had crashed and the fog was so thick they wouldn't be able to spot the wreckage unless they were right on top of it.

By noon the Montrose Search and Rescue Team was called and twelve members responded immediately. As they arrived, a lone Glendale Fireman climbing through the brush high at the top of the canyon heard a faint cry for help above him. As he gazed up the fog parted for just an instant and he spotted a plane's wing. The Fireman radioed his position, and began crawling up the near vertical mountainside, followed soon after by other Firemen and the MSR team. The last push was an 80-degree climb for over 800 feet.

Reaching the crash site, the fireman in the lead found the mangled fuselage with three people inside, all dead from massive injuries. The plane had apparently hit the mountain higher up and then rolled several hundred feet before precariously coming to rest. A few feet from the cockpit, a lone survivor lay on the ground, bloody, delirious and going into shock.

The team tied off the teetering wreckage to a tree to prevent it from sliding further. Using ropes, they raised a steel litter up to the crash site to carry the survivor down. They strapped him

These are the three boys that just happened to be hiking in Dunsmore Canyon when the plane crashed. If not for their quick action, the only survivor would have died.

This is what the crash site looked like, the plane teetering on a near-vertical slope and almost invisible in dense fog.

in for the long descent. The fog was so thick here they couldn't see each other, and had to shout commands to one another as they lowered the survivor down the near-vertical slope.

One of the MSR team members on the ropes was a doctor, and he became alarmed at the victim's condition. Blood was caked on the man's face, he obviously had internal injuries and many broken bones, and he was fading in and out of consciousness. He needed to get to a hospital quickly or he would die there in the canyon. The MSR team leader radioed a nearby Sheriff patrol helicopter to attempt a treacherous zero-visibility landing. Observers with radios were able to verbally guide the copter to a miraculous landing on a clearing in the canyon, and the men bearing the injured man gingerly descended to the waiting helicopter. The copter was one of the old bubble cockpit-style helicopters with no cabin for the injured man. The team wrapped the victim in blankets and strapped the litter to one of the helicopter's landing skids for the 10-minute ride to one of the few hospitals that had a landing pad back then (Verdugo Hills Hospital had not opened yet).

MSR team members stayed at the crash site with the dead bodies until FAA investigators got up the mountain. Just before sunset, they carried the three dead bodies back down the canyon to waiting coroner vehicles. The lone survivor, with multiple internal injuries, a broken back, leg and jaw, did recover. He had been saved from death by the Montrose Search and Rescue Team.

FINDING A CRASHED AIRPLANE ON CATALINA ISLAND

Because the Montrose Search and Rescue Team is so highly regarded, they are often called out to exotic locations far from home. Such was the case in February of 2009, when a small plane on a sightseeing run to Catalina Island disappeared on its way back to John Wayne Airport in Orange County. The Beechcraft Bonanza, with a pilot and two tourists aboard took off from Catalina's "airport in the sky" just before dark, but never showed up after the expected 20-minute flight to the mainland. Catalina's hilltop airport, a compact airstrip wedged onto a shaved-off mountaintop, is intimidating to many pilots, who equate it with landing and taking off from an aircraft carrier. To top it off, it was cloudy and raining the evening the ill-fated plane took off.

The Coast Guard searched the waters around the island all night but found no wreckage. In the morning, the call went out to the MSR team to assemble for helicopter transport to the island to search the rugged terrain around the airport. Because of the bad weather conditions, an air search would be impossible. It would have to be done on the ground. The cloud cover was nearly down to the water, so the rescue chopper was only able to drop the team off on a remote beach of the island. Two four-wheel drive jeeps from Avalon met them there and drove them into the back-country. MSR team member Mike Leum describes the search:

> We raced up the road near the top of the island and told the driver to stop. We got out and deployed our direction-finding equipment, which emits an audible beep tone when it finds the signal from the plane's ELT. [An ELT is an Emergency Locator Transmitter. All airplanes carry these small units, which transmit a radio beacon when they are turned on automatically by a sharp impact, such as a crash.]
>
> Not hearing any signals, we drove on down the road. Upon re-deploying the device, we got a hit. It was faint, and the signal was distinct. We sent the other Jeep carrying team members further down the road, and they also got a hit. These devices are direction-finding, so upon

Plane Crash Rescues

Rescuers hurry to bring out the only survivor of the plane crash.

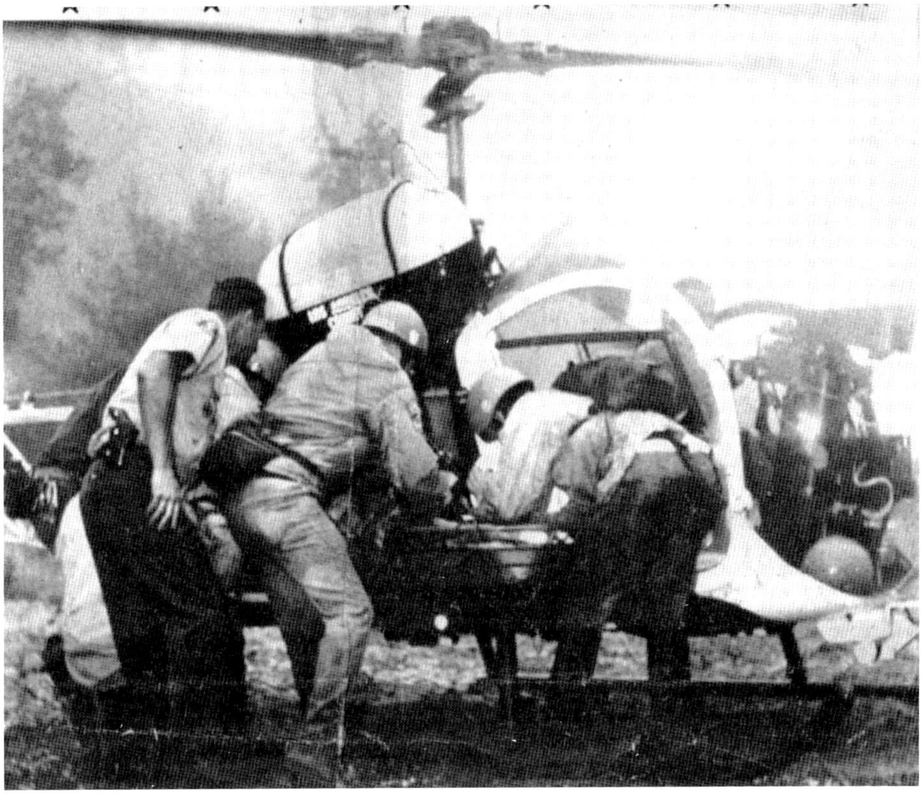

After making a miraculous zero-visibility landing, the small search helicopter waits as the team straps the victim to the outside of the helicopter.

The team is often called to far-off locations. Here they quickly assemble supplies for a multi-day search.

getting the compass bearings, we were able to narrow the search area. As we hiked on foot, the signal became stronger.

We broke into an all-out run, hoping to find survivors. For some reason, we always assume that we are looking for live victims, even though common sense would say otherwise. I swear, SAR members are the MOST optimistic people you will ever meet. We assume someone is alive until proven otherwise, even after a plane crash.

Then the smell hit us, the smell of burnt electronics. We came upon the fuselage, shrouded in fog. As we ran closer it appeared very unlikely that anyone could survive the inferno that had happened only hours before.[1]

The team found no one alive, only the charred bodies of the pilot and his two passengers. Their optimism had been in vain.

Mike continues:

There is a distinct smell of burned flesh that is like no other. It permeated the air. We weren't able to move the bodies due to the NTSB (National Transportation Safety Board) investigators needing to see the site, along with a homicide police unit which as a matter of protocol would also be responding. Lacking any survivors, our role was done, and we returned to the mainland, while Avalon Sheriff Deputies kept watch over the site.[2]

Mike Leum's description of the search illustrates the type of people that the MSR team is made up of. He describes them as being the most optimistic people you would ever meet, and that

Because crash sites are often in remote locations, the MSR sometimes takes responsibility for retrieval of the wreckage for investigators to look at. Here an aircraft engine has just been landed by helicopter.

they always assume that they will find survivors. And yet, when their hopes are dashed and they find only dead bodies as they often do, they are somehow able to recover, move on, and renew their sense of optimism for the next rescue operation. These men and women of the MSR are massively strong, not just physically, but mentally and emotionally as well. We have true heroes living amongst us in our peaceful valley.

---

1. Leum, Mike, interview by author.
2. Ibid.

This wreckage, retrieved from a crash site on Mendenhall Peak in the San Gabriel Mountains shows how wadded up the lightweight aircraft get when they crash.

After retrieval by helicopter, the wreckage is strapped to a trailer for transport to a site where investigators can pore over the twisted metal to determine the cause of the crash.

Underground Rescues

MINE RESCUES

Besides all the amazing "above ground" rescue services the Montrose Search and Rescue Team performs—finding lost hikers, snow rescues, wildfire rescues, cars and motorcycles off the mountain roads, and finding crashed airplanes—they also have a mine rescue team, currently the only full team in the state. (Other areas have composite teams, made up of volunteers and professionals from a variety of groups. MSR is the only mine rescue team that has remained as a unit throughout its nearly forty years of activity.) As a result, the Montrose team is in demand state wide, and many of their rescues involve travel.

You might ask, why a mine rescue team in Montrose? We're not known for our mining history. But a little-known fact of our mountains is that there are probably 100 mines within hiking distance of the Crescenta Valley. Not just gold mines, but water mines, all dug in the late 1800s and early 1900s. Water mines work like this: as rain soaks into the mountainsides, the water travels underground downhill until it either enters the water table or comes to the surface as a spring. But quite often it gets dammed up behind earthquake faults that run along the mountain range. The early settlers found that they could dig a horizontal tunnel into the mountainside, and when that tunnel pierced the fault line, the dammed-up water behind it would gush out, to be collected at the mine entrance. Most of these water mines were abandoned with the advent of gas and electric well pumps in the teens and '20s, but the Crescenta Valley Water District still collects water today from one of these old mines.

Every canyon of our mountains has at least one of these old abandoned water mines, and many have several. After the Station Fire denuded Dunsmore Canyon a few years ago, four open water mines were revealed, mines that had been hidden for a century by poison oak and brush. Over the years these dangerous open mines have attracted kids and curious adults to explore them. It was probably this that motivated the MSR to jump at the chance to train in underground rescue when the state offered the training in the early '80s. They were schooled in the use of oxygen and gas detection devices, the use of air tanks, ventilation, and the methodology of shoring up unstable cavities.

Since those early training sessions, the MSR has found a whole new world of applications for their talents. In an urban area like Los Angeles, underground tunnels are everywhere. Flood

This was the Montrose Search and Rescue team's underground rescue crew when they first formed in the 1980s, one of the first dedicated groups to do so.

control tunnels, utility vaults, aqueduct and sewage tunnels, open cavities beneath freeways and bridges, and subway train tunnels. As well, in earthquake-collapsed buildings, unstable tunnels are formed in the rubble that can be approached with many of the same methods used in old mines. As well, the oil-rich land beneath Los Angeles vents methane and hydrogen-sulfide gases that make underground work even more dangerous. In many cases the team has ended up rescuing other rescuers that responded to the initial calls for help, but rushed in unprepared.

Here are a few samples of the calls the mine rescue team has responded to: In 1991, an off-road motorcyclist went missing in Riverside County, in an area infamous for the many open vertical shafts that dotted the landscape. The MSR team used ropes to rappel down several likely shafts but didn't find the biker's body. He was never found.

In 1992, the team responded to a cave-in of a working gypsum mine in San Diego, where an equipment operator was trapped in the cab of a mine train. About 200 tons of the soft gypsum buried the train, and the MSR tunneled through the soft material, shoring up as they went. They rescued that miner alive.

One of their more complicated rescues took place in 2012 in Anza-Borrego, where a hiker had gotten trapped and died deep in some naturally occurring mud caves. Because his body was wedged tightly in a narrow passage, the team had to tunnel to the body from above and below using air-hammers to excavate enough room to extract the deceased explorer.

Obviously, claustrophobia is not an option for this hard-working far-ranging team.

A fully-equipped MSR underground rescue team member approaches the entrance to an abandoned mine.

Once inside the mine they wear oxygen masks as they string communications wires.

Above: Although we think of underground rescues occurring mainly in mines, construction sites are also a place where victims can get trapped underground. Here the team trains for rescuing workers from a deep trench that has collapsed in a mocked-up scenario.

Below: A MSR team member is lowered into an open mine shaft in the desert to look for the body of a missing biker.

Above left: In a training session, the underground rescue team learns how to shore up an unstable tunnel.

Above right: A MSR underground rescue team member squeezes through a tight spot in an abandoned mine while participating in a training exercise.

A WATER MINE TRAGEDY

We're next going to cover a tragedy that took place in our valley relatively recently. Because of that, we'll leave out the names and locations surrounding the terrible event. We cover it here, not to bring up bad memories for the families involved, but to illustrate how dangerous these old water mines are. These old unstable tunnels are located in most of our canyons, and in many cases, are covered by decade's worth of brush. Once discovered, their draw is irresistible, and occasionally deadly. They should be avoided.

Two brothers that had grown up in the valley had made a hobby as kids of exploring the old water tunnels up in the canyons. One tunnel tantalized them. About 300 feet in, the roof had collapsed, forming a dam. Water collected behind this accidental dam, submerging the tunnel, and the brothers always wondered what lay beyond. As adults one of the brothers became part of the elite Air Force para-rescue team, highly trained in scuba diving and rescue techniques. The old curiosity about the childhood water mine, buoyed by his confidence in his diving skills, made him decide to take a stab at what was admittedly a very dangerous adventure.

The two men hiked to the mine entrance carrying a set of scuba gear. They crawled into the tunnel to the cave-in. The diver donned his gear and tied a line to himself to be tended by his brother. He climbed over the cave-in and entered the dark water beyond. Threading his way through fallen timbers and rocks, he crawled and swam approximately 185 feet, while his brother paid out line. When he finally reached an open cavity, he raised his head above water.

No one really knows what happened at this point. Perhaps his regulator was accidently knocked out of his mouth, or maybe he misread his oxygen sensor. What we do know is that he took a breath of air that was only four percent oxygen and immediately passed out face down in the water. Back at the entrance the brother noted that the line stopped moving, and pulling on it was fruitless. After what seemed an eternity, he called for help and the MSR mine rescue team responded.

They entered the mine but were stopped at the 300 ft. mark by the cave-in and the low oxygen levels, twenty-one percent at the mine entrance but 18.5 percent inside the tunnel. Ventilation fans were brought in to freshen the air. A word about oxygen: The normal air we breathe is twenty-one percent. At fifteen percent, dizziness begins, and at nine percent unconsciousness soon follows. At seven percent the air supply to the brain is shut off immediately. The air in the farther portion of this tunnel was four percent, the oxygen probably eaten up by the decaying wooden timbers.

Fortunately, an experienced cave diver and training officer for the Sheriff's dive team had been flown in. He struggled over the cave-in and followed the line into the water. The way was treacherous. He passed several air pockets but didn't find the lost diver. He finally cleared the murky dark water to a half-submerged portion of the tunnel. Keeping his regulator firmly in his mouth, he found the diver's body. After removing the diver's tanks, the body was carefully threaded back to the entrance. This same brave cave diver had to retrace the route a week later to retrieve the diver's gear.

It was a traumatic event for the community, who mourned and struggled with the loss of one of our own. Yet this same sort of tragedy played out just two years later in Cleveland National Forest. Two young brothers used scuba gear to dive into a submerged portion of a mine, emerged in an air cavity that again contained only four percent oxygen, and they too died.

Mines are dangerous places, but even more so water mines. They're all more than a century old, and they were sometimes dug by amateurs, unschooled in safe mine construction. Any kind of cave or mine exploration is not to be taken lightly, but exploring our local water mines should not be attempted at all.

The team checks their gear before entering an abandoned water mine.

ABANDONED MINE TRAPS BOTH EXPLORER AND RESCUER

The abandoned mines that honeycomb our San Gabriel Mountains attract adventurers like moths to a flame. These ancient holes in the ground, often held up by rotting timbers over a century old, can be death traps for those with inadequate equipment and training. The Black Jack Mine near Acton was just such a place.

Appearing as little more than a small hole in the side of a hill, this horizontal mine opened up to several large caverns. At the back of the tunnel, a 6 ft. by 6 ft. vertical shaft dropped 800 feet straight down, with several horizontal tunnels branching off at various levels. A father and son had explored the mine several times, and returned in April of 1998 to explore the vertical shaft. They tied off a rope to a timber at the top of the shaft and descended 400 feet. Climbing back out, they made the mistake of trying to use an ancient wooden ladder affixed to the shaft's side. The lighter son made it to the top, but the old ladder crumbled under the father's weight at the 150-foot level, and he fell fifty feet, breaking their safety rope and landing on a ledge. Injured and exhausted, he couldn't climb out, so his son left him and went for help.

Several County Fire units responded and began prepping the area for a complicated rescue. Lights were set up as it was getting dark, and ventilation units started pumping fresh air into the mine. One of the biggest threats in these old mines are pockets of deadly gases, so the firefighters are careful to monitor air quality. The Montrose Search and Rescue Team arrived, and two of their members were selected to join the team that would actually try to reach the victim. The MSR and the Fire units began to build a frame on which to anchor a rope, while another team lowered a remote camera down to the victim, who couldn't be seen from the opening. On the way down the camera showed that there were many rotting horizontal timbers bracing the shaft. The camera reached the trapped explorer 200 feet down, who was conscious and responsive.

One of the MSR team was harnessed up and began the long descent down the shaft, being lowered by hand. On the way down, he had to thread carefully in and out of the fragile horizontal timbers, so as not to knock them loose to fall on the trapped man below. He reached the victim, strapped him into a rescue litter, and the haul team above pulled him to the surface. He was transported to a hospital.

During this rescue, the main rope attached to the MSR rescuer contacted one of the rotten horizontal bracing timbers just fifty feet above the rescuer's head and shifted it out of place. If it fell it would strike him on its way to the bottom of the shaft several hundred feet below, maybe taking him with it. They had two options. They could lower another man to the dangling timber and tie it off, or they could drop another line away from the timber and the MSR man could shift his tether to that rope. They chose the latter option.

After a new line was lowered on the side away from the loose timber, the MSR man carefully moved to the new line on the opposite side of the shaft and tied off to it. He remained tied to his original rope as a backup in case the timber did fall and hit him. Very slowly the haul team began to pull him up, while another team tried to keep both lines from touching the barely intact beam. He managed to squeeze by the old timber without touching it and made it to the surface, a very lucky (and tired) rescuer. The MSR and Fire Department secured their equipment, and Public Works was called in to permanently seal the entrance to the treacherous mine.

This operation shows the danger the MSR faces in these old mines. They are proud to be one of the few SAR teams in California to be trained in underground rescue.

Left: The son waits anxiously outside as the team tries to rescue his trapped father in the mine.

Opposite above: The team works at a rescue similar to the one at the Black Jack Mine.

Opposite below: In this shot from a training exercise, this victim has just been rescued from a 1,000-foot shaft.

The hard-working underground rescue team pauses as they descend into an abandoned mine.

The Lighter Side of Rescues

HEIDI THE SEARCH AND RESCUE DOG

The idea of the MSR having a tracking dog to locate lost and missing persons seemed logical, but it never panned out as planned. This is the rather unremarkable story of Montrose Search and Rescue's brief foray into employing a scent dog in their activities.

In the mid-'60s the Montrose Search and Rescue Team relied on local service organizations for much of their major funding. The '50s and '60s were a golden age of community service organizations. In every community across America, there flourished fraternal groups such as the Masons, the Elks, Kiwanis, Lions, Knights of Columbus and Rotary. They provided important social and business networking outlets for the community, as well as supporting charities with their robust fundraising activities. They all funded the MSR at one point or another. One such group locally was the Crescenta-Canada Junior Chamber of Commerce.

The local Junior Chamber of Commerce, or Jay-Cees as they were commonly known, donated a four-month-old purebred bloodhound named Heidi to the MSR, along with a donation for food and keep. One of the MSR members took on the job of trainer.

According to one member of the team, Heidi's record in the field was not stellar. According to that member, Heidi never really found anyone, and did a much better job at tying up MSR funds in food costs and vet bills. Heidi's fifteen minutes of fame came in January of 1966, when her photo was placed dramatically on the front page of the Valley Times, beneath the headline "Valley Tot Vanishes, 100 Combing Area." The case was one in which a three-year-old boy had disappeared from his family's home in Sylmar. The large photo shows Heidi's handler holding an article of the missing boy's clothing up to Heidi's nose. Heidi is more concerned with the flash of the camera, a worried look on her face, and her tail tucked between her legs. True to form, Heidi did not find the toddler. (To be fair to Heidi, the boy's body was later found on the bottom of the family's unused pool, where it had been overlooked by previous searches.)

At this point it seems that Heidi's role with the MSR became something that she was better suited for—that of public relations. Heidi's droopy smile was often in the paper, and she was a fixture at all the MSR's public outreach events. She was often photographed gazing up at the camera through the multiple folds of skin around her eyes, her ears forward, as her handler accepted a check from one or another donating group.

Left: Community groups helped purchase Heidi to be an asset for the Montrose Search and Rescue.

Below: The team poses for a group shot with their newest member, Heidi the bloodhound.

The Lighter Side of Rescues

Above: Heidi seems more concerned with the camera's flash than her upcoming challenge as she is called on to track a missing child.

Right: As an item of the missing toddler's clothing is thrust in her face, Heidi looks a little perplexed.

Here Heidi does what she does best: community outreach. This photo-op with a cute kid did wonders for the MSR team's image.

Heidi played a critical PR role for the MSR when the county briefly explored the idea of disbanding the all-volunteer unit in favor of a professional search and rescue unit. The all-volunteer MSR fought the idea in favor of the community-based and community-oriented outfit they had always been. They used Heidi prominently in their campaign to "save" the MSR. Heidi's droopy face is shown under the caption: "How sad it is... The possibility of being out of a job if the Montrose Mountain Search and Rescue Team is eliminated may be responsible for the indescribably forlorn look on the face of JayCee Heidi, member of the team." The drive to save the volunteer status of the team was successful.

As Heidi continued with her fundraising efforts, a little Heidi coin-bank was produced and distributed to local businesses and schools, to buy cold-weather gear for the team. "Just like me! That's what Heidi is proudly saying about her likeness in the form of a bank." said one caption. "Puppy with a purpose" said another. A caption challenged readers to make sad-faced Heidi smile with a donation to the MSR.

Droopy-faced Heidi eventually retired from her role with the MSR, to a status that perhaps she was meant to be all along—a pet.

Another photo-op with a cute kid. A little girl feeds coins into a "Heidi bank." The donations were used to buy cold-weather gear for the MSR. The team relied then, as they do today, on donations from the community to buy their rescue equipment.

Above: Heidi moved seamlessly into her new role as a fundraiser for the MSR. "Heidi banks" for coin donations were placed in Montrose businesses, here being accepted by a store owner in a newspaper photo.

Opposite: Howard Meehan of Kimmel-Meehan's men's wear store in Montrose accepts a "Heidi bank" to place right next to his cash register.

The Lighter Side of Rescues

MSR SAVES ORPHANED CHIPMUNKS

A sheriff helicopter on patrol above the Angeles Crest Highway in April of 1981 spotted the burned-out hulk of an overturned car off the side of the canyon five miles north of La Canada. The Montrose Search and Rescue Team rappelled 500 feet down the cliff to the wreckage of the car and retrieved the body of the driver.

In the burned vegetation around the car, the MSR team found two chipmunk babies right next to the charred hulk, apparently orphaned by the fire from the flaming vehicle. They brought the two chipmunks back to the station. Both babies were so young that their eyes were still closed, and the team took turns feeding them goat's milk mixed with sugar and baby formula with an eyedropper. The chipmunks seemed to thrive in their new home, a plastic bowl with wood shavings and a knit wool cap for a bed. The chipmunks were to be released after they had grown, and the MSR team members affectionately named them Susan and Debbie after two new MSR recruits.

An MSR team member feeds one of the baby chipmunks sugar water with a dropper.

THE HORSE RESCUERS

In 1995, a horse and rider embarked on an unfamiliar trail in the Little Tujunga Canyon area. The trail got really narrow and steep, so the rider dismounted to lead the horse by the reins. The horse lost its footing, panicked, and fell backward down the embankment. It tumbled head-over-tail down the grade. Although miraculously uninjured, the horse landed in such a way that it couldn't get itself out of the ravine on its own.

The horse was tranquilized and the rescue helicopter came to its rescue. A special harness was rigged up and attached to the hoist usually reserved for humans. The sleepy horse was airlifted to a nearby ranch, where the rescue crew stood by to help the horse to its feet as the tranquilizer wore off.

A special harness was fashioned by the team to pick the horse up out of the narrow ravine.

The horse's owner comforts the frightened but uninjured animal.

The Lighter Side of Rescues

There's something you don't see every day. The tranquilized horse is being carried by helicopter back to its stable on the end of a rope.

Finally back on the ground, stable hands and the rescue team try to keep the horse upright as the tranquilizer wears off.

MONTROSE SEARCH AND RESCUE FATHER AND SON TEAM

In 2002, a son joined his father on the MSR. Fred Koegler had been on the MSR for thirty years when his youngest son Lyle decided to join him. Lyle had grown up with the idea of community service. His mom and Dad had both been career teachers and had volunteered for other jobs in the community. Lyle had just graduated from Cal State Los Angeles, and was entering his career as a forester, mapping and fighting back-country fires. Since he had grown up in the "family" of the MSR, he felt it a duty to carry on the family tradition. "It's that whole community service thing" Lyle said. "I've always been involved with the community. Besides, it's a blast getting up there on the mountain, and getting out there on the side of a cliff, knowing you're helping people. It's giving back to a community that's given me so much."

Proud father and longtime MSR team member Fred Koegler poses with his son, Lyle Koegler, who had joined the MSR team that he had practically grown up around.

THE FIRST WOMEN TEAM MEMBERS

Until the 1980s the Montrose Search and Rescue unit was a "boys club." But in 1981, two women, Debbie Longo and Sue Lapham joined the team. They both completed the hundreds of hours training required, and passed rigorous physical tests, the same ones that the men are required to pass. Longo served the team for five years before becoming a full-time sheriff deputy, but Lapham was a team member for many years and even served as Captain of the team.

Sue came to the world of search and rescue via a dramatic incident that happened when she was in high school. Her younger sister and a group of neighborhood kids were trapped overnight in a snowstorm on Mt. Lukens (recounted earlier in this book), and their lives were saved by the Montrose Search and Rescue Team. She remembered that night of terror, waiting in her family's living room. She watched the professionalism of the MSR team members as they gathered information, then set out into the cold night to save her sister. That memory stayed with Sue for the next decade as she went to college and then embarked on a career as an ophthalmic technician.

Sue was a youth leader at her local church when she asked the MSR to come and speak to the kids. It was at that talk that it occurred to her that she could do what the MSR was doing, that she could save lives just as her sister's life was saved. She asked the team if she could join, and they said of course, so she began her training. Besides the Sheriff Academy training in law enforcement, weapons use, and tactical training that qualified her as a reserve deputy, Sue completed extensive survival training, map reading, mountain climbing, rope usage, as well as memorizing the hundreds of square miles of wilderness that the team covers.

Sue was in fantastic physical shape already, employing running and weightlifting to keep in condition for her MSR work. But one of the most important lessons Sue learned from all her training was that physical strength and size was not as critical to search and rescue as training and skill was. In an interview Sue said, "Strength is not as important as proper technique. Doing it the right way allows either a man or a woman to perform any of the functions equally well." In fact, Sue's smaller size made her a natural for the Montrose Search and Rescue's elite mine rescue unit, one of the only ones in the state. It's here that Sue's slighter frame and mastery of finesse made her a standout in this specialized field of search and rescue work.

Sue Lapham became part of the family of the Montrose Search and Rescue Team, and even married a fellow team member. Over the years other women joined her on the team, and today it's no longer a boy's club. Women now regularly become members of the MSR, but Sue Lapham will always be known as one of the pioneers.

There's no doubt that our community is privileged to have heroes such as these among us. They serve a vital role in a town that's perched on the border between a major city and a vast wilderness area. They are volunteers, yet they perform professional-grade rescues on a daily basis. We, as a community thank these selfless volunteers. Thank you, Montrose Search and Rescue!

The Lighter Side of Rescues

Sue's first call-out was a grisly one. Here, she and another team member prepare to lift a headless body (covered by discarded couch-cushions) up out of Big Tujunga Canyon.

Above: The Montrose Search and Rescue team is truly a part of our community. Here they march in the annual Montrose Christmas Parade, carrying a load of little kids in their rescue basket.

Opposite above: Sue and her husband met while serving together on the Montrose Search and Rescue team.

Opposite below: Back in the 1980s, Sue poses proudly as a new member of the team.

Bibliography

Goldsworthy, Steve. Interview by author.

Leum, Mike. Interview by author.

Montrose Search and Rescue Team. Private collection. Email lasdmontrosesar@gmail.com for more information.